A Cathedrals Coffee & Tea Tour

THE GUIDE THAT REFRESHES BOTH
YOUR SOUL AND YOUR PALATE

A Cathedrals Coffee & Tea Tour

SIMON DUFFIN

Matador
9 Priory Business Park
Kibworth Beauchamp
Leicestershire LE8 0RX, UK
Tel: (+44) 116 279 2299
Fax: (+44) 116 279 2277
Email: books@troubador.co.uk
Web: www.troubador.co.uk/matador

ISBN 978 1783061 518

British Library Cataloguing in Publication Data.
A catalogue record for this book is available from the British Library.

Typeset by Troubador Publishing Ltd, Leicester, UK

Matador is an imprint of Troubador Publishing Ltd

Printed and bound in the UK by TJ International, Padstow, Cornwall

ACKNOWLEDGEMENTS

Thanks first and foremost to my wife Anita for her patience as I spent hundreds of hours at my computer screen editing this book, and many days absent from home enjoying the various visits. She did join me for a good few trips, though, and that explains why I use 'we' and 'us' in some chapters.

Thanks to the following friends and family who offered me hospitality, guidance and company through the year: Caroline Boyle, Gerald Cox and Lucia, Karina & Viktor Dancza, Les & Jan Duffin, Rachel Heyburn, Julia and Rupert Kerrell, Manda Hobson & Steve, Mike & Jan Shackleton, Andy Smith & Annette.

A big thank you to all the coffee shop and tea room owners, managers, baristas and other staff who took time to talk to me during my visits and to give feedback and updates on the draft reviews.

And thanks to all those volunteers who do the guided tours of cathedrals, and to those who sit for long hours at the cathedral welcome desks, especially to those who understood immediately the kind of stories and history I was after.

CONTENTS

FOREWORD

This book takes the reader on a whistle-stop tour of the UK's cathedrals, and then gives top tips for where to find great coffee, tea and cake nearby.

I visited 110 cathedrals in 89 different towns and cities across the UK, going into each building with a secular eye to bring out the highlights. These can be architectural, sometimes religious, but mostly they are just the best stories I think each cathedral told, often connecting to the history of the area or the country as a whole. So this guide does not attempt to be the authoritative compendium on UK cathedrals – it just tells some good stories, like the previous *Fancy a Cuppa?* books.

The coffee shops and tea rooms suggested combine top quality tea, coffee and cake with a bit of character, either from their owners, the building or the area they are to be found in. Where possible, they're within walking distance of the cathedrals.

Why combine cathedrals with a cuppa?

Some people have asked what on earth the connection is between cathedrals and good coffee or tea. Well, the personal response is that I love all three, so why not write about them? And, I don't know about you, but after I've spent an hour gazing at stained glass or musing over old monuments, I need a cuppa, whatever time of day it might be.

Cathedrals

I have used the broadest possible definition of cathedral to decide where to go on this tour. This meant not just visiting the classic mediaeval Anglican cathedrals like York Minster or Winchester Cathedral. It meant going to places that only have a Catholic cathedral; in Scotland, it involved visiting places where the Episcopal Church is based; in Stevenage, there is a Coptic Cathedral! And in cities like Birmingham, it meant seeing three or, in the case of Glasgow, four cathedrals, across various denominations.

In the Church of Scotland, there are no bishops these days, so officially there are no cathedrals, since the word is derived from the Bishop's Throne or cathedra. But I extended my definition to include towns like Dunkeld and Dunblane, where everyone speaks of the 'cathedral' and it would have been a shame not to visit such beautiful places.

On the other hand, I opted not to traipse around some of London's outer suburbs in search of Ukrainian or Belarusian Orthodox cathedrals, and omitted some of the other smaller denominations of the Anglican and Catholic churches.

I also chose not to include Bath, where the Abbey was once a cathedral, but is no longer; and did not visit Westminster Abbey, but that was also on grounds of cost to get in, whereas the Catholic Westminster Cathedral is included in the book.

The highlights I have picked from each cathedral will not satisfy an art historian, an architect or a theologian. Rather, they are designed to draw in the average visitor and maybe even attract those who would never normally set foot in such a place. They are based on my own observations inside each of the cathedrals, although very often with the help of the excellent guided tours offered.

For the Anglican cathedrals, I include a reference to how they deal with entrance charges or donations. Any 'prices' or suggested amounts are 2012 figures. No other denomination charges to enter their cathedrals.

Towns or cities?

There is an urban myth that having a cathedral means a place is automatically designated a city. Another misconception has it that all cities have a cathedral.

Actually it's the British monarch who grants city status, and although traditionally this would have gone to places where a cathedral was built, this is not always the case. In 2012, to mark her Jubilee, the Queen made Chelmsford, Perth and St Asaph into cities, so until then these were cathedral towns.

Kingston-upon-Hull and Southampton are two major cities which have no cathedral. And Rochester in Kent, although historically a city with a mediaeval cathedral, lost its city status when it merged into a Medway town.

Coffee shops

The coffee shops recommended are all independent, usually one-offs run by a family, a couple or an individual. I do not review any chains, simply because they lack the personal touch and the unique stories that so many independent coffee shop owners have.

On the whole, I look for the best quality coffee, for those coffee shops that some call 3rd wave, others call artisan. Some of these can be a bit preachy about how you're supposed to drink your coffee: it's one thing to steer away from the bitter, scorching coffee served up very often in the corporate chains; it's another to be told you can't have milk or sugar! Having said that, my test of a really good coffee is indeed whether or not I feel the need to add a sprinkle of sugar…

Not all the coffee shops get their coffee beans from expert micro-roasters round the corner. And don't forget, I was looking for coffee near the cathedrals, so was not about to travel 5 miles into the suburbs of a big city just because there was an artisan roaster there.

What struck me, though, is that it is actually easier these days to find a decent cup of coffee in most UK towns and cities than it is a good cup of tea…

Tea rooms

I see four basic categories of tea rooms in the UK today:

Contemporary: This is the new wave of tea rooms in the UK, trying to take tea to where coffee has gone in the last six or seven years. The focus is on loose-leaf tea, choosing a blend to match your mood, trying green or white tea as well as black (and I don't mean 'no milk' by that), and the art of how to make it (temperature, brewing time, equipment).

Vintage, retro: These are usually run by funky, slightly edgy young women. Many of them also serve up loose-leaf and stress the same issues as the contemporary tea room, but here the focus is also on décor and atmosphere, often harking back to the heyday of tea in the 1920s, 30s or 40s.

Historical: This is the tea room in the fantastic mediaeval building, the sort of place you want to bring the family for 'traditional' afternoon tea. Sometimes you get lucky, and they also focus on a quality cuppa. But sometimes these places just serve up tea made with tea bags. This is not necessarily a no-no for me. Some tea bags can be OK as long as the food is good or the setting is extra special. But I have walked out of such places when I discover that the best they do is a cheap, corporate brand tea bag you could buy in your local supermarket.

Caffs: Sadly, in some towns and cities, all you can find is a rather insipid tea made without enthusiasm by pouring boiling water over a rather weak tea bag. I long for the day when these places go out of business, or change their practices, because there is strong enough customer demand for something better. Mind you, some caffs do a good, strong 'builder's brew'…

It's much more common to see a 'coffee house' on the average High Street than it is 'tea room' these days. In some cases, these coffee houses are little more than caffs, but sometimes you will see that I pick a so-called 'coffee house' as the best venue to get a decent tea! It's very rare (I think only once in this book) that I'll go for a coffee in somewhere that calls itself a 'tearoom'…

But maybe this will change as the new wave of contemporary tea room marches on…

Closures and new openings

The stories to be told in most cathedrals will not change much from year to year (unless you're in Leicester, where they found Richard

III's bones, or Lisburn and Sheffield, where cathedrals were completely renovated in 2012).

The world of the small, independent coffee shop and tea room is – sadly – not as stable. Some of the venues reviewed have been around for decades, but others I had planned to include closed down completely in the last 12 months, in some cases too soon before publication of this book to seek out a replacement.

The good news for lovers of a good cuppa is that new venues are also popping up all the time. Where I've caught wind of them in time, I've dropped by to check them out for inclusion here. But sometimes they open up too late for me to revisit, for example in Bristol, Portsmouth and Derry/Londonderry – I'll just have to include these in a future book!

SOME FAVOURITES

Top 5 cathedrals

Durham – *I agree with Bill Bryson on this one: he called it 'the best cathedral on planet earth'!*

Salisbury – *This place has everything: architecture, stories, setting; there's even the old cathedral ruins.*

Southwark – *Fantastic stories linked to Shakespeare, Native American chiefs and more.*

Portsmouth – *More great stories, often nautical and some with tea connections.*

St Davids – *The most atmospheric setting, whatever the weather.*

Cathedrals with sporting links

Gloucester Cathedral – *the 'Gloucester Golfer' is depicted in the East Window.*

Liverpool Cathedral – *former Bishop Sheppard captained the England cricket team in the 1950s.*

Liverpool Cathedral – *there's an angel with a football rattle in one stained-glass window.*

Norwich Cathedral – *Norwich City footballers are carved in the misericordiae.*

Paisley Cathedral – *the patron saint, St Mirin, gave his name to the local football club.*

Cathedrals marking how morals have changed

Brecon Cathedral remembers *two 'spinster' sisters who died aged 22 and 27.*

Canterbury Cathedral remembers how *'the Pope allowed him to marry his father's cousin'* …

Ripon Cathedral – *women used to have to squeeze through a hole in the crypt to 'prove their chastity'.*

St Davids Cathedral – has a book of Welsh law which says: *"Dead fish in the ocean all belong to the King"…*

Cathedrals with unusual uses

Dornoch Cathedral – *horizontal gravestones used to measure cloth on market day.*

Kirkwall Cathedral used for a *weekly market once*; and during Cromwell's time for *stabling horses.*

St Asaph Cathedral – *used for housing horses and oxen* during Cromwell's time.

Stevenage (Coptic) Cathedral – *appears to be used as a basketball court sometimes!*

Cathedrals with literary links

Portsmouth Cathedral – character from *Dickens' Pickwick Papers* in a stained glass window.

Ripon Cathedral – *Lewis Carroll's Dad was a canon. Some choir stalls inspired Alice characters.*

Rochester Cathedral – *Dickens remembered.*

Southwark Cathedral – *Shakespeare monument.*

Winchester Cathedral – *Jane Austen remembered here and lived nearby.*

Cathedrals with musical mentions

Armagh Cathedral – *composer of 'Ding Dong Merrily on High' was a chorister.*

Londonderry Cathedral – *'Once in Royal David's City', 'All Things Bright and Beautiful' written by a former Bishop's wife.*

St Paul's Cathedral, London – *Sullivan (of Gilbert and…) buried in the crypt, along with Blake and Parry, who composed 'Jerusalem'.*

Wakefield Cathedral – the *writer of the 'Lambeth Walk' was a chorister here.*

Westminster (RC) Cathedral – *Elgar's Dream of Gerontius first performed here.*

Cathedrals with film sets inside

Durham Cathedral – *Harry Potter's school was based here.*

Ely Cathedral – *The King's Speech filmed its 'Westminster Abbey' scenes here.*

Gloucester Cathedral – *Harry Potter scenes filmed in the cloisters.*

Lincoln Cathedral – *filming of Dan Brown's 'Da Vinci Code'.*

St Paul's Cathedral, London – *filming of Harry Potter & Madness of King George.*

Cathedrals with an American angle (my top 5 of many)

Aberdeen Episcopal Cathedral – *Samuel Seabury made 1st American Episcopal Bishop; flags of 48 American states painted on the ceiling.*

Bury St Edmunds – *'Martha' of Martha's Vineyard was baptised here; Godspeed boat remembered in the cathedral gardens; Dames of the Magna Carta in the US funded the rebuilding of the tower in the 1970s.*

Chelmsford Cathedral – *memorial to US servicemen posted nearby; George Washington's arms; Department of the US Air Force crest; Thomas Hooker – founder of Connecticut was preacher here.*

Oban (RC) Cathedral – *exiled Highlanders in the US funded the build of the Cathedral.*

Southwark Cathedral – *Bruce Two Dogs Boszum, Chief Mahomet, buried in the cathedral grounds in 1735; Harvard was baptised here.*

Cathedrals with Australian tales

Dunblane Cathedral *roll of honour includes names of locals who fought under the Australian flag.*

Manchester Cathedral – *kangaroos carved in the Bishop's throne because a former Bishop had come from Melbourne.*

Northampton Cathedral – *Caroline Chisholm appears on the Australian $5 note; her funeral was in this cathedral.*

Perth Cathedral – *designed by the same architect as designed Adelaide Cathedral.*

The venues

Top 5 coffee shops

Coffee Aroma – Lincoln: *Where I first learnt what quality coffee is!*

Spring Espresso – York: *Great coffee, great couple running it & fantastic signature cake.*

Window Coffee – Norwich: *Small venue, top barista, great coffee and cake.*

Coffee House – Shrewsbury: *Great buzz to the place – family feel; top quality cuppa*

Flat Caps – Newcastle: *Great character, loves his coffee and so do I.*

(and close behind: Association Coffee – London; Monmouth – Southwark; The Plan – Cardiff; Strangers – Wells; Flat White – Durham)

Top 5 tea rooms

Peacocks Tea Rooms – Ely: *Like tea at someone's house, because that's where they live!*

Waterloo Tea – Cardiff: *The kind of contemporary tea room I'd want to run one day.*

Olde Young Tea House – Middlesbrough: *My favourite vintage chic tea room.*

The Tea House – Norwich: *Great to see guys rather than girls running a quality tea room & doing the baking!*

Charlotte's – Truro: *Must be the best tea room in the UK with its tea grown just 5 miles away…*

(and running them close: Tea Sutra – Newcastle; Moat Tea Rooms – Canterbury)

Top 5 venues for cake

Frou Frou – Enniskillen

lovecrumbs – Edinburgh

Spill the Beans – Dunkeld

Julie's Coffee House – Oban

Tea-Licious – Durham

I may be biased, but it seems they bake a better cake up north – must be the different temperatures…

Top 5 venues with a cathedral view

Manna Tea Rooms – Portsmouth: *Look directly out to the Cathedral through their main window.*

Peggottys – Rochester: *You're looking at the side wall of the Cathedral, but it's pretty impressive.*

One Eighty on the Hill – Armagh: *The Cathedral's straight across the road from the front room.*

Bea's of Bloomsbury – St Paul's: *You have to pick the right seat to get this narrow view of St Paul's.*

Harries Coffee – Arundel: *With views like this, who cares if it rains or shines on Arundel Station?*

Favourite 'other activities' on the premises

Riverdale – Inverness: *massage and other complementary therapies.*

Leakey's – Inverness: *Scotland's biggest 2nd hand book shop (in an old church).*

Zappi's Coffee – Oxford: *Bike shop.*

Browns Coffeehouse – Canterbury: *Punting on the River Stour.*

Shannons – Lisburn: *Jewellery firm.*

Bean there? – Hereford: *Map shop.*

Favourite venues for Twitter feed

@SokoCoffee – St Albans: *Cheery one-liners on Charlie's commuter customers.*

@Cafeat36 – Exeter: *A leading light on the Exeter independent retail scene.*

@Brewsmiths_JQ – Birmingham: *Another couple very much part of their community.*

@Cleverdickcoffe – Norwich: *Tweets on football and coffee, though this guy's a hairdresser!*

@FlatCapJoe – Newcastle: *Tweets on coffee and life in general.*

ABERDEEN CATHEDRAL CHURCH OF ST MACHAR

The 16th century heraldic ceiling is the highlight of this cathedral: all the big wigs of the day are commemorated: Henry VIII, of course, but also Charles V (he was King of Spain, Aragon, Navarra and Sicily, as well as Holy Roman Emperor, so his head appears five times); and Louis was King of Bohemia and Hungary. Ah, the world was a different place then!

Best story here must be the 'Scottish Samurai', Thomas Glover. He was a local engineer who made good in Japan, founding Mitsubishi. His family grave is in the cemetery, but he is buried in Nagasaki.

This is Church of Scotland, so don't go looking for the cathedra. There are no bishops in the Church of Scotland, so in fact this is not officially a cathedral...

The 'parliamentary clock' hanging on the south wall dates from the 18th century – it was so-called because public service clocks could avoid paying the extraordinary – and short-lived – Clock Tax, imposed by act of parliament in 1797.

Recommended donation of £2.

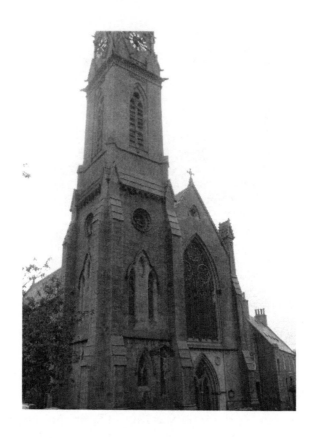

ABERDEEN CATHOLIC CATHEDRAL – ST MARY'S

The Millennium Murals up by the altar show Scottish saints through the centuries. Most intriguing were the 9 MacDonald Maidens, who were apparently missionaries near Abernethy in the 8th century.

The city patrons mural depicts Aberdeen from mediaeval times through to the modern-day harbour and customs house.

The lists of local bishops have exotic-sounding names like Nectanus (1131-32) and Eduardus; the gap between the 1500s and the 1700s is as telling as ever; and there's the restored Catholic hierarchy in 1878, 28 years later in Scotland than in England.

No recommended amount for donation.

ABERDEEN EPISCOPAL CATHEDRAL – ST ANDREW'S
(locked on Monday, the day of our visit)

In 1784 in the Long Acre Chapel, Samuel Seabury was consecrated as Bishop of America for the Anglican Church. There's a memorial window in Seabury's name.

The coats of arms of 48 US states are painted on the vaulted ceiling of the north aisle. The two missing from today's 50 states? Alaska and Hawaii.

Coffee?

Kilau Coffee

59 High Street, Aberdeen AB24 3EH
www.kilaucoffee.wordpress.com

Open

Monday – Saturday

It's a shame the local roasters MacBeans don't serve a cuppa in their central Aberdeen store. But the nicest part of town anyway is Old Aberdeen with the mediaeval university and its cobbled streets. And right in the middle of that is the best coffee shop in town, a stone's throw from the Cathedral.

Tea?

Richmond Street Deli

65 Richmond Street, Aberdeen AB25 2TS
www.richmondstreetdeli.co.uk

Open

Monday – Saturday

Just a short walk from Aberdeen's grey granite centre is the Rosemount district of town, with its independent shops and community feel. There you'll find this friendly little café where you can get a good pot of loose-leaf tea and feel a part of that community.

ALDERSHOT CATHEDRAL OF THE ARMED FORCES
(CATHOLIC)

The trowel and mallet used by Queen Victoria to mark the start of work on this church in 1892 are displayed now in the main entrance to the Cathedral – they're a bit flashier than your average garden tool, though!

There's a replica sculpture of Our Lady of Lujan on the window ledge by the Verger's office: left behind by Argentinian soldiers after the Falklands conflict, it was presented to the Catholic priest of the troops in 1982 and now gifted to the Cathedral in Aldershot.

Look at how many memorial plaques show how soldiers used to die of disease or 'illness contracted while on service' rather than in military action, especially before penicillin was discovered.

The old church bell now sits under the Victoria trowel and mallet display – it was in danger of crashing through the roof otherwise; HMS Invincible's bell is also within the Cathedral.

No mention of donation amounts; in fact the church is only open for mass on Wednesdays and Sundays, though visitors can always knock on the Verger's door and he's very willing to open up!

Coffee?

Caffe Macchiato

7 Union Street, Aldershot GU11 1EG
www.caffemacchiato.com

Open

Daily

A good community coffee shop often has work by local artists on
the wall, but how often is the artwork by the owners of the coffee
shop themselves? This is our top tip for Aldershot, but not just
for the décor: it's also the best coffee we tasted in town.

Tea?

Sadly, we didn't find anywhere we can recommend for tea in
Aldershot.

ARMAGH CATHEDRAL OF ST PATRICK'S
(CHURCH OF IRELAND)

Look at the list of Abbots & Bishops in the North West corner of the Cathedral. First up, in 444AD, was Patrick. Yes, that's THE Patrick, patron saint of Ireland, though historians are less certain on the exact dates he was around.

If you enjoy singing "Ding Dong Merrily on High" at Christmas, you might like the plaque commemorating Charles Wood, the composer who did the arrangement for the carol – he was a chorister here.

This is Ireland's Cathedral HQ. St Patrick himself decreed that this place should hold sway over all other churches and monasteries in Ireland.

The oldest objects in the church date from 3,000 years ago, though: one is of the Tandragee Man; the other they're not sure about, but some say it's a topless queen from the Bronze Age (with horse-looking ears, though…)

7

The Bramhall Chair, up by the altar, is a beautiful 17th century antique in its own right. But its story also marks key events in history: made in 1660 (year of the restoration of the monarchy); it was then removed a hundred years later and then re-discovered in a London antique shop in 1922.

Brian Boru, King of All Ireland, is buried in the graveyard outside. Been there since 1014!

There's an admission 'fee' of £3 to enter this cathedral.

ST PATRICK'S CATHEDRAL, ARMAGH
(ROMAN CATHOLIC)

This cathedral may be a lot newer than its Church of Ireland counterpart, but it has by far the best views over Armagh, from the top of the tiered staircase leading up to the entrance.

The story goes that Sandy Hill was the place to which St Patrick brought a deer and fawn, when his mates wanted to kill them. That's why the Cathedral was built here, and the story is depicted in the great East stained-glass window.

The Archbishop here is the Cardinal of All Ireland. Armagh's diocese ignores Ireland's man-made boundaries; and when the Cathedral was re-dedicated after major renovation work in 2003, Ireland's President Mary McAleese attended, even though the church is strictly speaking in the UK!

A window in the north wall depicts Armagh's two cathedrals side by side.

Don't miss the rather unique altar: 21st century; made from Tunisian limestone, and totally symmetrical. How did they know which side to have facing the congregation?

Donations 'for Cathedral upkeep' but no amount recommended.

Coffee/Tea?

One Eighty on the Hill

4 Vicars Hill, Armagh BT61 7ED

www.oneeightyrestaurant.co.uk
(website for their Portadown branch)

Open

Tuesday – Saturday

Tea room or coffee shop? Whichever you call it, this is surely the best in Armagh. And it's perfectly-placed opposite the Cathedral; it's all in a good cause, helping young people with learning disabilities into traineeships and employment in catering…

ARUNDEL CATHEDRAL OF OUR LADY AND
ST PHILIP HOWARD

The Cathedral was designed by a Mr Hansom, who also invented the Hansom cab – his remit here was to make it fit in alongside Arundel Castle.

> There's a memorial plaque to Bernard Cuthbert Taylor, a local lad who had the misfortune to be a 3rd class steward on the Titanic. During our visit, there was also a temporary exhibition about him and the job he signed up to do without knowing the consequences!

St Philip Howard's remains are to be found here, along with a shrine to this former Earl of Arundel who was one of 40 English and Welsh martyrs made saints in 1970 (though he actually lived in those turbulent years of the 16th century when signing up to the 'wrong' religion could mean you lost your head).

> The Glossop family's tribulations are marked on plaques remembering one Glossop dying in action in South Africa in 1900 and two younger brothers dying in First World War trenches (1916-17).

If you're at all unfamiliar with Saints Days, there's a wonderful book displayed along the South Aisle, with highlights from the year and explanations of why the person became a saint. For the week we were there, it was St Catherine of Alexandria, who was famously killed on a spiked wheel; then St Andrew, who became patron saint of Scotland – so you know when we were there, don't you?

There's also a full register of deaths going back to 1860, but with the names listed by day of the year. It's always open on the day in question, but you are free to leaf through (though treat it with care – this book has been here for 150 years).

A simple message by the exit says the Cathedral needs funds for upkeep and 'we'd be grateful if you could make a donation'…

Coffee?

Harries Coffee Bar

Arundel Station, Arundel BN18 9PH

www.harries-food.com
@harriescoffee

Open

Monday – Friday (until the 9.12am train leaves!)

Rain or shine, Heather will serve you up a steaming cuppa and some toast if you want it before you leap onto your train from Arundel Station. And if you're driving past Arundel early morning, this coffee is worth taking a little diversion for – it's only a short hop from the A27 and there is plenty of free parking.

More coffee later?

Gaskyns Café

4-6 Queen Street, Arundel BN18 9JG
www.gaskyns.co.uk

Open

Daily

Good coffee and fantastic cakes in this spacious building that was originally part of a massive brewery by the river in Arundel and then part of a cinema. Now it's a friendly family-run coffee shop with lots of space for community groups to meet.

Tea?

Belinda's

13 Tarrant Street, Arundel BN18 9DG
http://www.arundel.org.uk/dining/belindas/

Open

Daily

Tea has been served in this 16th century barn since the 1920s. It's a stone's-throw from the picture-book mediaeval castle and the Cathedral. The scones here are something special, and they let you choose whether it's whipped or clotted cream...

AYR CATHEDRAL – ST MARGARET'S

The 14 Stations of the Cross portraits are rather unique, though one local we spoke to thought they'd be better off in Tate Modern. We quite liked them; but it's true it's hard to tell which is which…

The building is locked much of the time, largely due to break-ins and thefts! Try turning up an hour before the daily mass at 10am if you want a look around, and they stay open a little longer on Tuesday/Wednesday mornings, apparently.

No recommended amount for donations.

Coffee?

Pandora Coffee House

32 New Bridge Street, Ayr KA7 1JX

www.pandoracoffeehouse.co.uk
Facebook: Pandora Coffee House

Open

Daily (but shorter hours on Sunday)

This coffee shop in the centre of Ayr has kept the original 1920s light fittings from when it first opened as a family-run Italian café. Owners Jan and Tom have run Pandora since 1979, moving in to this old café in 1985. Best coffee we had in Ayr, and great Scotch pancakes – home-made, of course.

Tea?

Sadly there is nowhere in Ayr we can recommend for tea.

BANGOR CATHEDRAL

A cathedral was first built on this site in AD546.

The quilt covering the nave altar depicts various aspects of local life, with pieces of slate embroidered into the fabric; there's even a picture of a now de-commissioned nuclear power station...

The Bishop here speaks Welsh, as well as English.

Mediaeval slate quarry workers made donations of a penny each to begin restoration work on the Cathedral.

Just by the Cathedral shop stands the 15th century wooden carving of a pensive Christ, before his crucifixion.

No recommended amount for donation: "What you can afford".

Coffee?

Blue Sky Café

Ambassador Hall, Rear of 236 High Street, Bangor LL57 1PA

www.blueskybangor.co.uk

Open

Monday – Saturday

Fancy supporting a co-operative made up of 12 North Wales tea rooms that have signed up to fair trade, quality produce and locally-sourced goods? Well, this is a good place to start, just off Bangor's High Street: it's the best coffee and cake you'll get in town.

Tea?

Bangor Pier Tea Rooms

Garth Pier, Bangor LL57 2SW

Open

Thursday – Sunday

You won't find better value tea and scones anywhere in the UK. Vic has had his hands in the scone mix for over 53 years and as soon as he sees supplies getting low, he'll pop another batch in the oven. Fantastic spot for a tea room, too, down the end of a pier reaching far out into the Menai Strait towards Anglesey.

BELFAST CATHEDRAL OF ST ANNE
(CHURCH OF IRELAND)

This cathedral has two bishop's thrones, facing each other up by the altar: for the Bishop of Connor and the Bishop of Dromore.

The enormous spire is a recent addition (2007) in a very lightweight material because of the soft foundations risking the whole building sinking into the river!

Look for the prayer book made by prisoners of war in Korea in 1953 out of rice paper (for cigarettes), ink given for writing home, and a cover made from pillow cases wound over cardboard.

George Berkeley, whose name inspired the college in California, was a local guy and his face looks down on worshippers in the nave.

Photos at the back of the Cathedral show how close it came to being bombed in World War Two.

Don't miss the Coventry Nails posted on the east wall; donated from the rubble of Coventry Cathedral after it was bombed in WW2 – the nails are 600 years old.

The US flag commemorates the first US troops to disembark in Europe during World War 2 – in Belfast, of course.

Donation of £2 recommended

BELFAST ST PETER'S CATHEDRAL (CATHOLIC)

Designed by a priest who had been trained as an architect; the land was bought by a successful baker in the 19th century – it's now hemmed in close to residential streets of west Belfast.

Don't miss the bust of Archbishop Cahal Daly (Primate of all Ireland from 1990 to 1996).

The Holy Oils are kept in a display cabinet dedicated to two priests who were killed at the height of the Troubles in the early 1970s.

No recommended amount for donations.

Coffee?

California Coffee

43 Arthur Street, Belfast BT1 4GB

www.mycaliforniacoffee.com

Open

Monday – Saturday (open Sundays also in run-up to Christmas)

The two brothers who run this coffee shop learnt their trade in San Francisco's coffee bars about 13 years ago. There are traces of California all over this place AND they serve up the best coffee in Belfast, we think.

More coffee?

Upperlands Coffee

at St George's Market, Belfast BT1 3NQ

www.upperlandscoffeecompany.com

Open

Saturday – Sunday only (at the market in Belfast)

John and Julie Henderson learnt about coffee while running a farm in Massachusetts, but they've been roasting coffee in the farming area of Upperlands for some ten years now, with great results, and serve up great coffee from their stall in Belfast's St George's Market at the weekends.

Tea?

Maryville House Tea Room

2 Maryville Park, Lisburn Road, Belfast BT9 6LN

www.maryvillehouse.co.uk
@maryvillehouse1

Open

Daily

This Victorian Gentleman's Townhouse down the Lisburn Road makes a perfect setting for a relaxing afternoon tea in Belfast. Lovely loose-leaf teas on offer and a good range of cakes and scones. And if you really like the place, why not stay the night at the B&B?

Afternoon Tea?

The Great Room Restaurant, The Merchant Hotel

16 Skipper Street, Belfast BT1 2DZ

www.themerchanthotel.com

Open

Daily

This may have once been the HQ of the Ulster Bank, but it works well now as an elegant hotel with The Great Room a fantastic place for afternoon tea, taking you back to the mid-19th century, when Belfast was thriving on trade and Empire.

BIRMINGHAM CATHEDRAL – ANGLICAN (ST PHILIP'S)

This is the place for pre-Raphaelite fans, with four windows by Burne-Jones (East and West).

Two characters stand out among those with named plaques:

Peter Oliver, who was Lord Chief Justice of Massachusetts when the 'calamities' struck in 1776. He remained loyal to the Crown and died in exile in Birmingham.

Edward Thomason, who died in 1849 as a knight of Great Britain, Prussia, Persia, Naples, Spain, Netherlands, Sardinia, Portugal and Belgium – how did he manage that??

Also worth looking for: the memorial to the victims of the 1974 pub bombings in Birmingham (in the cathedral gardens); and the bell of HMS Birmingham (under the west window).

Recommended donation of £3.

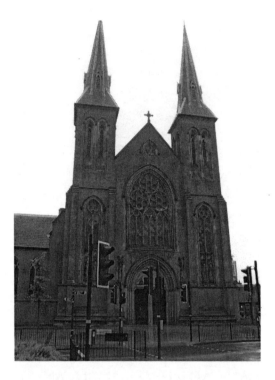

BIRMINGHAM CATHEDRAL – ROMAN CATHOLIC
(ST CHAD'S)

A section of the ceiling is marked with a plaque showing where a
bomb entered through the roof in 1940 (amazingly it did little
damage!).

Relics of St Chad are stored above the High Altar in St Edward's
Chapel.

The organ is the largest entirely mechanical organ in the Midlands
(built 1990s).

No recommended amount for donation.

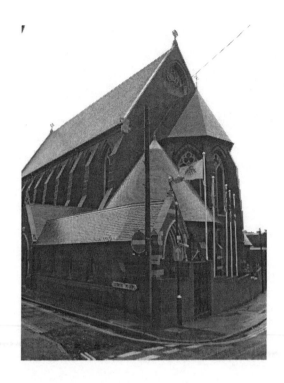

BIRMINGHAM CATHEDRAL – GREEK ORTHODOX

This is the classic bright church, all chandeliers and icons, with beautiful yellow and brown brickwork.

All signage inside is in Greek, except for the words 'Tea Room' – out the back, tables were laid, but I guess this is only used after services are held...

No sign of any box for donations, let alone recommended amounts.

Coffee?

Six Eight Kafé

6/8 Temple Row, Birmingham B2 5HG

www.sixeightkafe.co.uk
@sixeightkafe

Open

Daily

With coffee from one of our favourite coffee roasters in the country (Has Bean) and tea from those great blenders based in Belfast (Suki), Six Eight is our top pick for a cuppa in Birmingham – great spot to people-watch in the nation's second city, too!

More Coffee?

Saint Caffe

61 St Paul's Square, Birmingham B3 1QS

@SaintCaffe
www.saintcaffe.com

Open

Monday – Saturday

There are lots of messages in this coffee shop, set on the beautiful St Paul's Square, that aim to educate the people of Birmingham on the best way to drink coffee. With a chief barista known as @TheHolyBarista, you might think they're a bit preachy, but these guys just want everyone to enjoy the best in their coffee. If you want it YOUR way, just tell them!

Tea?

Yorks Bakery Café

1 Newhall Street, Birmingham B3 3NH

@YorksBakeryCafe
www.yorksbakerycafe.co.uk

Open

Monday – Saturday

We loved the fact that the owner of Yorks Bakery sends his tea expert to China every year to meet the growers and suppliers directly, including an intriguing set of monks from Fujian Province! Their coffee and cake are pretty good too, but we gave them top marks for tea.

More tea?

Brewsmiths Tea and Coffee

214 Livery Street, Birmingham B3 1EU

Facebook: Brewsmiths
@Brewsmiths_JQ

Open

Monday – Saturday

Best place in Birmingham for a bacon butty and a warm welcome on a winter's morning. Makes me almost wish I commuted into Birmingham's Snow Hill Station round the corner from Brewsmiths. Of course, they're in our book because of their loose-leaf tea and excellent cakes, too!

BLACKBURN CATHEDRAL

A German POW (Siegfried Pietsch) carved the gold figures that stand over the west door and south entrance.

The stained glass windows range from spectacular 1990s design (in the tower) through pre-Raphaelite to one 600 year-old window from the original Early English church on this site.

Turn around as you enter at the West Door:- see the sculpture of Christ the Worker, with tools from the various Blackburn-based industries.

Look for the Red Roses on the door into the chapel dedicated to local soldiers who died in conflict.

A small sculpture of the Virgin Mary was modelled on a local lass who was seen standing at a bus stop by the sculptor – now an elderly lady, this model still attends services today.

Look for the trademark 'mouse' on the wooden lectern from Yorkshire sculptor Robert Thompson.

In the cathedral gardens, look out for the remaining pillar of the mediaeval church; and for the family tomb of former PM Robert Peel.

No admission charge here – recommended donation is £3 and there weren't many coins in there when we threw in ours...

Coffee?

Exchange Coffee Company

13-15 Fleming Square, Blackburn BB2 2DG

www.exchangecoffee.co.uk
@exchange_coffee

Open

Monday – Saturday

This is one of those local coffee roasters that used to be on every High Street in the land. If you time it right, your nose will bring you in. Great quality hot drinks all round, so not just the coffee, and some lovely home-baked cakes, including Lancashire Parkin.

Tea?

Hartley's

70 Northgate, Blackburn BB2 1AA

Open

Tuesday – Saturday

Go back in time to the days when music really rocked, and the two ladies (twins) who run this place used to boogie on down to The Beatles and Elvis in the local dance hall. Lots of 50s and 60s paraphernalia on the walls. And these girls bake a mean cake, with tea from the local roaster/blender Exchange, so it's great quality.

BRADFORD CATHEDRAL

Look out for the sheep carved in the Bishop's Throne: Lambs of God or symbols of Bradford's wool trade? Or both? And the mention of St Blaise, patron saint of the wool trade (apparently he was flayed with wool combs).

Anglican Cathedral, on a site where Christian worship began in 627AD, with missionaries arriving here from...Dewsbury!

During the Civil War, woolsacks were hung around the tower to protect it from Royalist artillery.

Don't miss the William Morris designed windows; or the 1724 oak ceiling.

Memorial stones to interesting local pioneers: industrialists and chemotherapy researchers.

The Cathedral today has eco-solar panels; no wonder it's so warm inside in winter!

Donations box so discreet it's hard to find. They don't want it to ruin the welcome the Cathedral wants to give to people.

Coffee?

Smorgasbord Coffee Bar

2/4 Rawson Place, Bradford BD1 3QQ

www.smorgasbordcoffeebar.com
Facebook: Smorgscoffee
@smorgscoffee

Open

Daily

Slap bang in the middle of Bradford's shopping district, this coffee shop serves up the best coffee we found in Bradford. And owner Arif has a classic Bradford story to tell: father came to work in the mills in the 1950s, Arif went to uni and got a taste for coffee culture, which he has now brought back to Yorkshire!

Tea?

Tree House Café

2 Ashgrove, Great Horton Road, Bradford BD7 1BN

www.treehousecafe.org
Facebook: Treehouse Cafe

Open

Monday – Friday (11.00am – 2.00pm)

Back in 1994, this was the UK's first totally fair trade café. And it's a workers' co-op even today, so don't start asking who's in charge round here! But there's a very relaxed feel to the place, with great cakes to go with your cuppa and a shop downstairs where you can even buy Zapatista Coffee from Mexico!

BRECHIN CATHEDRAL

There's an 11th century Irish-style Round Tower attached to the south-west corner of this cathedral, one of only two in Scotland. Used originally as a bell tower and for safekeeping of manuscripts and relics.

A plague stone leans against the base of the Round Tower inside the Cathedral. It seems that two thirds of Brechin's population died in a four month period in 1647 ("Four risings of the moon, saw 600 slain by the plague" – though 600 was generally used to mean 'a lot').

There are several framed 'Cradle Rolls' listing all children baptised in the Cathedral, dating back to 1906 – what's not clear is whether a name crossed-out meant they had later died or left the parish; but the practice seemed to stop in the 1910s.

They think the St Mary Stone, on the wall by the font, dates from the 9th century. It was found in 1782, as confirmed by the graffiti of the date carved into the stone, presumably by its finder…

Any donation gratefully accepted – various leaflets cost a nominal sum (40p for the walk round guide!).

Coffee?

Rosie's Bakehouse

26 High Street, Brechin DD9 6ER

Facebook: Rosies Bakehouse

Open

Monday – Saturday (plus brunch on the 1st Sunday each month)

Rosie's really put her stamp on this place, with her excellent baking. But she's also keen to connect to the past of this building, which was the home of the city elders in 1768 and then a bakery from 1856. But look out for the child's shoe on the mantelpiece: there's a story behind that as well…

BRECON CATHEDRAL OF ST JOHN THE EVANGELIST

The tapestry in the Weavers and Spinners Chapel was made to mark the church's 900th anniversary. It depicts one scene from each of the nine centuries, from plague, through battles, to the contemporary jazz festival in Brecon.

The Cresset Stone by the entrance would once have been filled with oil or candle wax and used to light the path for monks to worship at night; believed to be the only one in Wales and the largest in the UK.

Dr Who has signed the visitors book in the past – note his residence (and that of his sidekicks): Tardis (see the display along the north wall).

Sign of changing times (and use of language): Sybill and Hester Prosser were two 'spinster' daughters of the town grocer who died at the age of 22 and 27 respectively. Spinsters, indeed! (plaque on south wall).

Don't miss the 13th century chest, crudely carved out of hard wood, in an age before the trade of joinery had been invented.

There is no fee to enter; visitors are simply asked to make a 'generous donation'…

Coffee?

Gegin Fach

6 Market Arcade, Brecon LD3 9DA

Open

Monday – Tuesday; Thursday – Saturday

The name of this social enterprise coffee shop in Brecon means 'Little Kitchen' in Welsh. Great place for a cuppa, but there's nothing little about the home-baked cakes they serve up too.

Tea?

Pilgrims Tea Rooms

Brecon Cathedral, Brecon LD3 9DP

http://www.pilgrims-tearooms.co.uk/index.php

Open

Daily

A great value cuppa and cake at this tea room right on the cathedral grounds in Brecon. We particularly liked the photos of old Brecon on the wall, and loved the way this new build blends in with the mediaeval structures all around.

BRENTWOOD CATHEDRAL

It's the chandeliers that catch the eye first: there are 22 of them in a design typical of buildings modelled on Sir Christopher Wren's style.

Look closely at the congregation's chairs: they're all 'Essex chairs', from a time when each county had its own design. Essex chairs have 3 or 4 balls in the back frame.

The Stations of the Cross were made by the man who drew the Queen's head for the current set of coins. A modern design, quite hard to work out which is which, and note there are 15 rather than the usual 14 (there's an extra one for the Resurrection).

Check out the drawing/map of the whole diocese, stretching from Stratford and the Olympic Park in east London, to Harwich, and from Saffron Walden to Southend – it's in the narthex as you enter.

The original church on the site dates from 1861; part of it is still there and now makes the Blessed Sacrament chapel of the Cathedral.

No recommended amount for donation; just a small slot for 'cathedral upkeep'…

Coffee?

Rossi

17 High Street, Brentwood, Essex CM14 4RG

Open

Daily

This is the place to hang out for coffee in Brentwood and you can bring the kids for a home-made ice-cream and a photo opp with Mr Licky outside...

Tea?

Marygreen Manor

London Road, Brentwood, Essex CM14 4NR

www.marygreenmanor.co.uk

Open

Daily (for afternoon tea)

Henry VIII, Katharine of Aragon, Samuel Pepys, the Wright Brothers. Just a few of the celebrity names who may well have had a cuppa here before you. It's a classic venue for a stylish afternoon tea in England with lots of history.

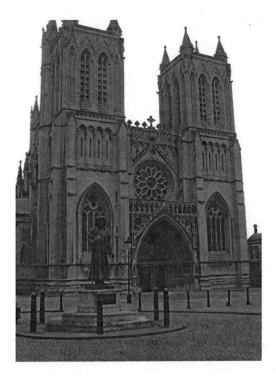

BRISTOL CATHEDRAL (HOLY & UNDIVIDED TRINITY)

The Chapter House dates from 1165 and is still stunning today, with its Norman curves and its red stone; it used to hold the Cathedral's library until the Bristol riots of 1831 when crowds, angry at the then Bishop's opposition to electoral reform, tried to burn the place down, but only managed to destroy the book collection.

The windows in the north aisle depict services like the Home Guard and Red Cross who protected communities during the World War, but is it just me or does one of the Wardens look a bit like Hodges from Dad's Army?

The oldest artefact in the Cathedral? Probably the Saxon Stone, which pre-dates the Cathedral. It was found under the floor after they were cleaning up following the 1831 riots and fire.

In contrast, there's some striking 1960s art in the window at the east end of the south quire – all dramatic reds, greens and blues.

There's an old stone staircase that used to be used by the monks when they'd come down from the dorm at night into the abbey; trouble is modern health & safety rules have forced the Cathedral to cover it with sturdy wooden steps – you can still see the stone… just!

Sir John Young's tomb is intriguing. Made in 1606, it is very colourful and decorated, but why is only his wife shown in the sculpture? Surely rare that a figure with that much wealth and influence should choose not to have himself portrayed in perpetuity…

How often do local journalists get a memorial plaque in a cathedral? John Latimer was a 19th century editor of the local paper, but also a local historian. His memorial refers to his 'beautiful character' – shame he isn't still talked about so widely.

Entrance to the Cathedral is free – so buy one of their excellent guides for £3.50…

BRISTOL CATHOLIC CATHEDRAL (ST PETER & PAUL)

Built in the 1970s, this cathedral is one of those concrete blocks that were so popular in that period; it was done 'on the cheap', costing a mere £800,000 to build from scratch.

The Stations of the Cross are very distinctive; they were made in fibre glass directly into the drying concrete: do none of the human characters have ears? And if not, why not?

Step inside and your eyes are drawn immediately to the two coloured glass windows. 8,000 pieces of glass set in a resin – they represent 'Pentecost' and 'Jubilation'.

The seating appears at first like lines of chairs in a relatively comfy village hall, but the layout is designed to make sure nobody is more than 50 feet from the altar.

No recommended amount for donation. There's a guide you can buy for £1, but it could do with an update...

Coffee?

Baristas Coffee

29 Victoria Street, Bristol BS1 6AA

@BaristasBristol

Open

Monday – Saturday

Opened on a whim in 1999 because the owners just left college and liked good coffee, this place must now be one of the longest surviving of the new wave of independent coffee shops in the UK. Still serves up great coffee and owner George is as passionate about it as ever.

Tea?

Lahloo Pantry

This was one of the best contemporary tea rooms in the country, but very sadly it closed down at the end of May 2013. The owner's great-great grandfather had sailed a tea clipper, so tea is in the family's genes, and we're sure they will reopen somewhere in town before too long.

We didn't get a chance to revisit Bristol in time, but we hear good things about:

Cox & Baloney

182-184 Cheltenham Road, Bristold BS6 5RB

Tel: 0117 944 3100

http://www.coxandbaloney.com/

Open

Tuesday – Sunday

Lots of loose-leaf and various afternoon tea menus in this vintage tea room attached to a vintage clothes and furniture shop on one of the main roads out of Bristol.

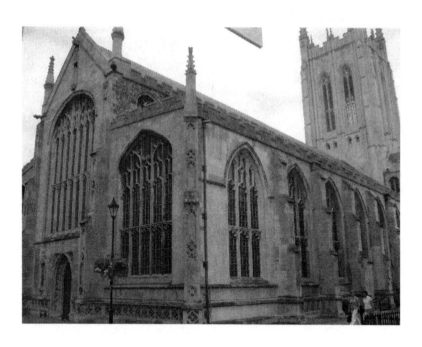

CATHEDRAL OF ST EDMUNDSBURY

Come to the Cathedral at Bury St Edmunds and you'll also want to visit the enormous grounds and ruins of the Abbey that used to dominate the town; the Cathedral is the former St James parish church, part of that complex.

The Martha who gave Martha's Vineyard its name was baptised in the cathedral font here; she died aged two but her father was one of the early arrivals in America; he also helped found Jamestown, in Virginia.

The whole tower in the centre of the Cathedral was only built in 2000; the 'extension' to the Cathedral – from the end of the nave onwards – dates from the 1970s, and was part-funded by the wonderfully-named Dames of the Magna Carta in the US.

Spot the 'lieutenant chairs', where The Queen and Duke of Edinburgh sat when attending the Maundy Money service a few years ago.

See the sculpture of the Godspeed boat that took early settlers to America in 1606.

The kneeling cushions on all the pews bear the names of the 600 or so parishes in the diocese of Bury St Edmunds.

No recommended amount for donation – just a statement that donations 'help cut costs'! Excellent free guided tours.

Coffee?

Really Rather Good

31 Abbeygate Street, Bury St Edmunds IP33 1LW

www.rrgood.co.uk
@reallyrgood

Open

Daily

This place not only serves up the best coffee in Bury in our view, but it has the prime location right opposite the entrance to the magnificent grounds of the Abbey. We rather liked their sniff box, too, in case you fancied a tea and can't decide which one to choose!

Tea?

Harriet's Tea Rooms

57 Cornhill, Bury St Edmunds IP33 1BT

www.harrietscafetearooms.co.uk

Open

Daily

You can see why lots of Americans drop into this tea room in Bury St Edmunds for a 'truly English experience'. It all looks wonderfully Edwardian, but friendly and helpful as well, with a lovely pot of loose-leaf tea to wash down those scones, jam and cream...

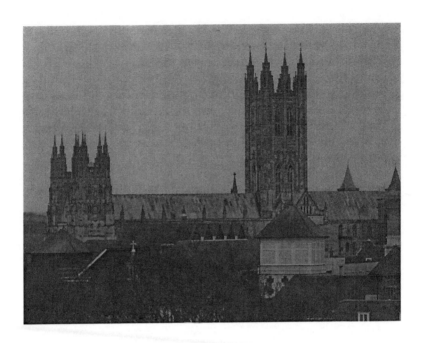

CANTERBURY CATHEDRAL

The Martyrdom is the part of the Cathedral where Thomas a Beckett was murdered in 1170. At some point in recent history they dropped his 'a', and the shrine today refers only to 'Thomas'. Next thing you know it'll be just 'Tom'. But this is what has made the Cathedral a place of pilgrimage for hundreds of years.

Don't miss the Disney-style 1950s stained-glass windows in the southeast transept. The designer did indeed study at the same school as people who went on to draw for Disney.

A 1480 wall painting has survived the centuries (and Henry VIII/Cromwell) in extraordinary condition. It depicts the legend of St Eustace, with pirates, lions, wolves and relatives being roasted to death.

There is a Calvinist Church within the Cathedral dating from the 16th century when Walloons and Huguenots came to Kent for asylum; they still hold weekly services here today.

Simon Willard is commemorated in a plaque on the south wall. He died in 1676 having been sent to America as Commander-in-Chief of British forces against 'hostile Indian tribes'…

In another fascinating sign of how our morals and laws have changed over the centuries, one memorial refers to how 'the Pope allowed him to marry his father's cousin'. I wouldn't want to marry my Auntie Sylv, but I certainly wouldn't need the Pope's permission today!

Admission fee (even to the grounds) is £9.50 (2012 prices); and you pay a further £4 for an audio tour or £5 for a guided tour.

Coffee?

Willows Secret Kitchen

42 Stour Street, Canterbury CT1 2PH

www.willowstree.co.uk
@willowscoffee

Open

Daily in summer (closed Sundays in winter)

Great coffee here from the wonderful Has Bean and All Press roasters. The guys who run this place – and all their baristas – are passionate and knowledgeable about their coffee. It's a cosy little place. And if you're into vintage vacuum-brewed coffee, this is a must for you in Canterbury.

More coffee?

Browns Coffeehouse

Water Lane, off Stour Street, Canterbury CT1 2NQ

@BrownsCoffeeHse
Facebook: Browns Coffeehouse

Open

Daily

Sit and watch the river flow by as you sip on your coffee; or in summer opt for a punt (yes, really – tickets available at the bar!). Quality coffee and locally-baked cakes in this lovely coffee shop right next to the tourist information office and heritage museum in Canterbury.

Tea?

The Moat Tea Rooms

67 Burgate, Canterbury CT1 2HJ

www.moattearooms.co.uk

Open

Daily

So many great stories to this tea room in the heart of Canterbury: from the timber-fronted building, through the family who run it with such passion and enthusiasm; to the great quality tea, packed and blended only a few miles away in Kent. A wonderful place for tea and cake.

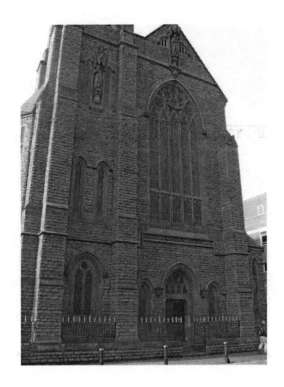

CARDIFF METROPOLITAN CATHEDRAL (RC)

The Catholic Cathedral in the centre of Cardiff was destroyed in an air raid in 1941, so the current one in the same street dates from a rebuild in the 1950s.

There's a memorial to the Welsh-Italians who died when the SS Arandora Star was sunk in 1940. This ship was taking Italian and German civilians who lived in the UK to Canada – the memorial shows the name of each Welsh town next to the person who had been living there.

Another memorial refers to the two Cardiff martyrs who were hung, drawn and quartered for their beliefs in 1679 in the Roath district of the city.

No amount recommended for donation.

LLANDAFF CATHEDRAL OF ST PETER & ST PAUL

The first cathedral in Llandaff was built around AD560. Llandaff means 'Church of the Taff' – the Taff is the river that runs nearby.

After a landmine hit the Cathedral on 2 January 1941, only the Lady Chapel could be used until the church was rebuilt in 1958. A memorial stone marks the spot in the garden where the landmine fell; it is made from stones of a cottage that was destroyed in the blast.

The bronze carvings of wild flowers in the Lady Chapel are named in honour of the Blessed Virgin. Marygold becomes Gold Mair in Welsh; but Buttercup is Mary's Sweat; and Foxglove Mary's Thimble in Welsh.

The Celtic cross is the oldest thing in the Cathedral – they were lucky it was found at the back of a shed in 1870!

Fans of Burne-Jones' pre-Raphaelite work should not miss the porcelain panels in the Dyfrig Chapel.

For lovers of more modern art, check out the goldfinches flying by the portrait of Gabriel, with his Teddy Boy looks and very distinctive red torso...

No amount recommended for donation, so why not buy one of the pamphlets giving a guided tour of the place. They need more than £1,000 a day to maintain the Cathedral.

Coffee?

The Plan Café

28-29 Morgan Arcade, Cardiff CF10 1AF

http://thebeanvagrant.com/
@TheBeanVagrant

Open

Daily

A beautiful coffee shop in a Victorian arcade in the heart of Cardiff. Fantastic quality coffee, always in-season and roasted by some of the best UK roasters. But the best thing of all here? A top barista who recognises that not all customers want their coffee the way the text books say they should...

Tea?

Waterloo Tea

5 Waterloo Gardens, Penylan, Cardiff, CF23 5AA

http://www.waterlootea.com/
@WaterlooTea

Open

Daily

I loved everything about this tea room, from the range of top quality loose-leaf teas on offer, to the fantastic home-baked cakes and the contemporary décor. They even do master classes in tea from time to time. And their coffee isn't bad, either!

More tea (nearer the Cathedral)?

Jaspers Tea Rooms

6 High Street, Llandaff, Cardiff CF5 2DZ

http://www.jasperstearooms.com/

Open

Daily

Take afternoon tea in what could be the 2nd oldest building in Llandaff. It's just a short hop from the Cathedral itself (the oldest building), so you're likely to be competing for a seat with vergers, choristers or coachloads of visitors on a busy weekend afternoon.

CARLISLE CATHEDRAL

The original cathedral, built around 1100, had running water underneath; during a period of drought some years later, the main tower began to sink – see the extraordinary buckled arches inside if you really want to witness subsidence…but this place has survived!

There are beautiful mediaeval paintings on the choir walls painted onto wood; these are south-facing paintings protected by a large curtain now.

Check out the 16th century graffiti in the choir, and the 18th century signatures carved into the cope chest along the north wall.

See the standards for the local Border Regiment going back to 1750; they've certainly seen some action over the years.

Check out the carvings about 12 feet up on the columns at the east end of the church; each carving represents a month of the year.

See the scorching from centuries of candles lighting up the choir.

An Augustinian Priory was part of the original cathedral complex; you can have a cuppa in the Fratry where the monks would have lived: Prior's Kitchen is open from 9.45am – 3.30pm daily.

No admission charge but a recommended donation of £5, well worth it if you get a tour by one of the knowledgeable members of staff here.

The Venues

Coffee?

Foxes Café Lounge

18 Abbey Street, Carlisle CA3 8TX

www.foxescafelounge.co.uk
@foxes_cafe

Open

Tuesday – Saturday

Music's always been important to the guys who run this Carlisle coffee shop. The previous owners have gone south with their band to try to make it in the music world. The current team in charge are making this a bit of a community hub, with gigs, open mic nights and films of local interest, as well as good coffee, of course.

More coffee?

John Watt & Son

11 Bank Street, Carlisle CA3 8HG

www.johnwatt.co.uk

Open

Monday – Saturday

This old Victorian grocer's has retained the atmosphere and décor of a hundred years ago. They blend their own teas and the former owner even comes back to grind the house coffee too. Quality cuppa whether you have tea or coffee.

Tea?

Bobbin Coffee Shop

Linton Tweeds, Shaddon Mills, Shaddongate, Carlisle CA2 5TZ

www.lintondirect.co.uk/the-bobbin-coffee-shop.html

Open

Monday – Saturday

Linton Tweeds have been weaving and selling their fabric to the designers of Paris, Milan, London and New York for over 100 years. Now you can have a cuppa and a home-baked cake in the tea room attached to the mill and study the history of the place while you sip your tea, or join the local knitting group if you can time your visit right.

CHELMSFORD CATHEDRAL

Anglo-US friendship is marked in the South Porch, with memorial stones for the US servicemen who were based in the area between 1942 and 1945; there's a stained glass window with George Washington's arms and another with the Department of the US Air Force.

Don't miss the steel memorial with the names of the workers from Hoffmann's ball bearings factory, who were killed while at work during bombing raids in the War; the plaque was put up when Hoffmann's closed down in 1989.

Thomas Hooker, founder of the American state of Connecticut, is also remembered, as he was the preacher round here before he escaped to America to avoid persecution for his Puritan views.

Most colourful object in the Cathedral is the Mildmay memorial.

Dated 1571, it commemorates Thomas Mildmay and his wife Avice. The plaque is in Latin but even the translation is eloquent: "They had 15 pledges of their prosperous love, seven whereof were female, and eight were male".

The altar cloth in the Mildmay Chapel depicts the journey of St Cedd in AD653, starting on Holy Island (Lindisfarne), going through Yorkshire and ending up at Bradwell and Tilbury in Essex.

No recommended amount for donation; in fact, I needed to ask where to place my donation since there was no obvious urn or container...

Coffee?

Buscall & Flynns Tearoom & Cakery

74 Springfield Road, Chelmsford CM2 6JY

www.buscallandflynns.co.uk

Open

Daily

A great example of women in business trying a new venture, this place opened only a few weeks before we turned up at the end of 2012. Nice cuppa from Taylor's of Harrogate (coffee or tea) and some delicious home-baked cakes. We wish these ladies luck...

Tea?

Small Talk Tea Rooms

25 Springfield Road, Chelmsford CM2 6JE

www.smalltalktearooms.co.uk

Open

Monday – Saturday

A fascinating blend of central Europe (the owners and the tea) with olde worlde English (the décor). Not many Brits know about the Czech tea traditions, so get along here and find out more.

CHESTER CATHEDRAL

The cloisters are the highlight here: check out the saints (with handy saints day dates) and other dignitaries in the stained glass windows; and the beautiful gardens in the centre.

Thanks to World War 2 bombings, there are now beautiful new stained glass windows in the main west window (1960s 'summer of love' theme) and the south windows (1992 design known as the Westminster windows).

Don't miss the cobweb picture, painted on the web of a silkworm in the 18th century.

The elephant and castle carving in the quire is pretty good given that the sculptor had never actually seen an elephant!

Imagine yourself on trial at the Consistory Court, or perched on high as the court usher...

Frederick Phillips is remembered here because he 'opposed, at hazard of his life, the late rebellion in North America' – this around 1776 of course...

Henry VIII's people missed the ceiling carving of Thomas-a-Beckett – make sure you don't.

Entrance fee £6 – comes with audio guide but there are no real people to take you round.

Coffee?

The Barista's Coffee Shop

9 Watergate Street, Chester CH1 2LB

www.thebaristas.co.uk

@thebaristasches

Open

Daily

There's a good vibe to this coffee shop in Chester, not just because of the friendly family-run atmosphere and the quality coffee, but also due to the history of this building, which was the only place in Chester to remain free of the Plague in the 17th century! It's called 'God's Providence House'.

Tea?

Katie's Tea Rooms

38 Watergate Street, Chester CH1 2LA

www.mdsrestaurant.co.uk/katies.html

Open

Daily

There's loose-leaf tea with home-made scones in this 14th century merchant's house a stone's throw from Chester Racecourse. If they gain their Grade 1 listed building status, this could be the only tea room in England in such a historic house.

CHICHESTER CATHEDRAL OF THE HOLY TRINITY

The first cathedral round these parts is now under water. It was in Selsey until 1070, when they began building in Chichester. Who said the oceans only began to rise with global warming?

When they installed the central heating system in the 1970s, they discovered that the 12th century cathedral builders were not the first construction workers on this site: there's a small patch of Roman mosaic flooring now revealed under the south aisle.

The spire used to be used as a navigation point for approaching ships until the whole thing collapsed in 1861. There's an extraordinary photo of the rubble after the fall in a display by the info desk; nobody died and it was rebuilt in five years.

The Tudor paintings in this cathedral are epic. One was a grand portrait of Henry VIII with his Dad and below that a portrait of English kings going back a few centuries – this was an unsuccessful attempt to save the Cathedral from ransacking at the hands of Henry's henchmen.

Get ready for a blast of red as you stand behind the altar. In the north east corner of the Cathedral is the vivid red stained glass made by Chagall when he was 91 years old; at the back of the altar is a dramatic tapestry depicting the miracles of St Richard.

Don't miss the memorial plaque to Gustav Holst (set in the floor) and the rather over-sized statue of a Mr Huskisson, who became famous for being the first person ever to be killed by a train (Stephenson Rocket, actually, driven by George Stephenson himself in 1830). But he was MP for Liverpool so why the big statue here?

Fans of Philip Larkin will rush to the Arundel tomb to check how true it is that love will survive us – are the earl and his countess holding hands? Was it the sculptor's intention? Read Larkin first!

Francis Chichester sailed single-handed round the world in the 1960s, but he was from Devon, not this part of Sussex. Is it just because of his name that Chichester Cathedral has the Gypsy Moth IV flag?

They found a finger bone in France in the 1990s, which apparently came from St Richard, so they were able to re-establish the shrine to him which had been here until Henry VIII's days.

This cathedral wants the place to be open to people of all faiths and none, so it is free to enter. They recommend a donation of £5, well worth it, especially if you take one of the daily guided tours.

Coffee?

Attibassi

1C Church Square, Chichester PO19 7BD

www.attibassi.com
Facebook: Attibassi Chichester

Open

Daily

The Romans brought a bit of Italian culture to these parts 2,000 years ago. Now this new coffee shop has brought a bit of Italian coffee culture to Chichester in the 21st century. Best coffee we could find in town!

Tea?

St Martin's Tea Rooms

3 St Martin's Street, Chichester PO19 1NP

www.organictearooms.co.uk

Open

Monday – Saturday

The story of these tea rooms goes back to 1975 when a young man decided to buy up an old Georgian house and convert it into an organic tea room. That young man is still around today, with the same principles, but an enthusiastic and friendly team running the show now and still serving up top quality tea and cake. A must if you're in Chichester.

CLOGHER CATHEDRAL – ST MACARTAN'S

There's been a church on this site for 1,500 years, and you can feel it the moment you walk through the gate away from the main road into the cathedral grounds. Wonderful peace and light inside.

The Clogh-Oir is a Golden Stone which gave the village its name, and it is thought that the large stone standing in the Cathedral entrance is the original Stone; it is one of three Stones of Erin, used in pagan times as an oracle (another stands in Westminster Abbey).

Another stone dates from the 7th century. It stands now in the Cathedral porch, with a replica marking the entrance to Clogher from Belfast.

The main path through the churchyard was once the bridleway to Dublin; heads off past the fort of Rathmore Hill.

No recommended amount for donation.

The venue

Tea?

The Station House Coffee Shop

The Station House, Augher BT77 0AX

Open

Daily

If you can't reopen old railways very easily, the best you can hope for is that someone converts the old station buildings into a coffee shop or tea room. At Augher's beautiful old station, just two miles from Clogher Cathedral, that's exactly what new owners Nick and Jackie have done. Great value pot of tea and scone!

COVENTRY CATHEDRAL OF ST MICHAEL

Is there anywhere else in the world where the bombed-out shell of one cathedral merges with a 1960s modern-build? And small bits of the original 11th century cathedral are just round the corner too.

For memories of the November 1940 bombings, see the charred cross made from beams that fell and burned in the fire (the original is in the modern building; a replica in the old); see the reconciliation sculpture among the ruins; and spot the Churchillian Victory V in the plumb-line sculpture inside.

The tapestry behind the altar is the size of a singles tennis court – the biggest in the world.

The Bishop's Throne is an extraordinary modern piece of furniture, with a canopy of nuts and bolts to represent Coventry's former industries.

Lots of 1962 memorabilia: 1962 penny coins in the floor for the processions up the aisle; check out the Private Eye front cover from the week the Cathedral opened; and the images of the 5 continents in the Unity Chapel floor somehow have the feel of an end-of-empire period...

For the blind, there is a model of the new and bombed-out Cathedral, with audio commentary to take your hands on a virtual tour.

There is an obligatory £8 entrance fee to this cathedral (and it's only valid for multiple visits in a year if you Gift Aid, so hard luck you overseas visitors...).

Coffee?

Kahawa Coffee

163 New Union Street, Coventry CV1 2PL

Facebook: KahawaCafe
@kahawa_cafe

Open

Monday – Saturday

Surely the best coffee in Coventry. This place only opened at the end of 2012, but young owner Bally has a good business head on him and has started well by recruiting an excellent barista and using quality coffee beans.

More coffee with some cake?

Conroys Coffee House

59 Corporation Street, Coventry CV1 1GX

www.conroyscoffeehouse.co.uk

Open

Monday – Saturday

Coventry was one of the hardest places in the country to find a decent cuppa, so we were pleased to come across this place just between the historic Spon Street and the concrete malls of the centre. Lovely home-made cakes by a lady who knows a thing or two about baking.

Tea?

Sadly, we didn't find anywhere we can recommend for tea in Coventry.

DERBY CATHEDRAL OF ALL SAINTS

The oldest part of the Cathedral is the tower, dating from the 1500s. You walk through this space as you enter the church so make sure you look around as you do!

Bess of Hardwick's memorial is the star attraction: she began life as a servant girl, but ended it as Countess of Shrewsbury and owned Chatsworth House when she died.

Fabulous choir screen in wrought iron – made by local ironmaster Robert Bakewell.

Note the shepherd's crook hanging on one wall – marking Derby's link to the farming communities.

No admission charge and no suggested amount.

Coffee?

Jack Rabbits

50 Queen Street, Derby DE1 3DE

www.jackrabbitskitchen.co.uk

Open

Daily

Best place for a cuppa with views of the Cathedral. This gourmet deli has fantastic cakes and bread as well as good coffee, and owner Amelia is passionate about making sure everyone's happy.

Tea?

Duesbury Restaurant – Royal Crown Derby

194 Osmaston Road, Derby DE23 8JZ

www.royalcrownderby.co.uk

Open

Monday – Friday

This is the place to come for a bit of Derby history. They've been making beautiful china at this factory for over 130 years. You'll not only have your tea served on Royal Crown Derby, but you can see the replica tea sets to those made for the Titanic 1st class passengers, and be tempted by the £1,000 plates usually sold to rich Sheikhs.

DERRY/LONDONDERRY – ST COLUMB'S CATHEDRAL (CHURCH OF IRELAND)

During the siege of Londonderry in 1689, protestants defending the town used the cathedral tower to aim their mortar fire at James's Jacobite troops; in the entrance to the Cathedral is a mortar shell which was fired into the city during the siege, but it contained surrender terms rather than explosives (the terms were rejected).

Famous hymns such as 'Once in Royal David's City' and 'All Things Bright and Beautiful' were written by a former Bishop's wife Cecil Frances Alexander – there's a window to remember her; but she is buried on a 'Green Hill With Out the City Walls'...

In the Chapter House Museum are the enormous padlocks and keys used to lock the city gates when the Apprentice Boys first closed the doors on James's men.

Don't miss the 1798 Union Jack hanging in the South Aisle, easily spotted because it is missing the red diagonal cross of St Patrick (that was added only in 1801).

The stone marking the completion of the Cathedral in 1633 still stands in the wall of the entrance porch: "If stones could speake, Then London's prayse should sounde…"

£2 'admission fee', although the sign was covered by a box as I left the church and there was no 'ticket office' to buy your entrance.

ST EUGENE'S CATHEDRAL (CATHOLIC)

The decision to build this cathedral was taken only a few years before the potato famine ravaged this part of Ireland, so although the foundation stone was laid in 1851, there wasn't a lot of money around to complete the church until 1873.

At the west end of the North Aisle is a stained glass window depicting St Columba blessing Derry – but can you see any identifiable landmark that defines this as Derry?

The Irish version of this cathedral's patron saint, Eugene, actually translates as 'Born under the protection of the yew' – I wonder how many Genes from America realise that…

No recommended amount for donation so why not fork out £2 for the excellent guidebook?

Coffee?

Java Coffee Shop

33 Ferry Quay Street, Derry BT48 6JB

Open

Daily

This is the place to come for a decent coffee with home-baked scones and home-made jam right by Derry's famous city walls and a stone's throw (if that's the right terminology here...) from the Church of Ireland Cathedral.

Tea?

Our favourite tea room in Derry closed shortly before we published this book, after 25 years under the same owner.

We are hearing good things about a new venue in Derry, serving quality tea and coffee, but we have not yet been ourselves: Warehouse No 1, Guildhall Street, Derry BT48 6DD.

DORNOCH CATHEDRAL

In 1570, most of it burnt down after a battle between the Murray clan and the Mackays, but we're pleased to report that the two families are so reconciled now that if you look at the woven choir cushions, you'll see the osprey design was made by a Murray and the puffin by a Mackay.

They display a copy of the Cathedral charter on the wall. Dated 1223-1245. Of course the Church of Scotland has no bishops so this is no longer officially a cathedral, but everyone knows it as such.

Madonna had her baby baptised in the Cathedral before getting married to Guy Ritchie in Skelbo Castle, nearby.

Don't miss the gravestones laid out flat so that traders on market day could measure their lengths of cloth correctly.

That great sponsor of education, Andrew Carnegie is remembered in the series of stained glass windows in the quire.

Look out for the 'mortality stones' dotted around the church, depicting various symbols of death, including skull & crossbones. Most date from the 1700s.

No recommended amount for donation – a very welcoming cathedral & they even offer you a coffee if you arrive for the service on Sunday!

Coffee?

Luigi's

1 Castle Street, Dornoch IV25 3SN

www.luigidornoch.com

Open

Daily

Not only does this place serve up the best coffee in Dornoch, but if you sit outside on a fine day, the chances are you'll get to see half the town walking past and most of them will greet you with a cheery hello. Great home-baked cakes, too.

Tea?

Royal Golf Hotel

The First Tee, Dornoch, Highlands IV25 3LG

www.royalgolfhoteldornoch.co.uk

Open

Daily

If you're into golf, this is our top tip for a spot of tea at the 19th hole, and if you're the long-suffering partner of a golf fanatic, this is the place to come anyway. You get great views not only of the 1st tee but of the long sandy beaches beyond. A place to dream the afternoon away.

DOWN CATHEDRAL

Ireland's patron saint is presumed to be buried under the present Cathedral, but in the 19th century a commemorative stone was placed in the churchyard and is today known as St Patrick's Grave.

The 10th century font, right in front of you as you enter, was lost for hundreds of years. It was found in Denvir's Hotel, just down the road and returned when the Cathedral was rebuilt in the 1800s.

Patrick was actually a privileged Brit (from Northumbria or thereabouts), who was kidnapped by Irish in the early 400s and sold off as a shepherd slave in Ireland. It's his conversion to Christianity and his subsequent escape to France that led ultimately to his becoming one of the most well-celebrated saints on these isles.

Interesting lay-out of the pews, either facing each other across the nave (this was originally a Benedictine Monastery) or in boxes, where whole families could sit together for services.

Go through to the annex to the shop to find paintings showing the ruined monastery and the Cathedral as it was designed to look when the architect was appointed in 1787.

Strong recommendation of a donation of at least £3.

Coffee?

Market Street Café

29-31 Market Street, Downpatrick BT30 6LP

Facebook: Market Street Café

Open

Monday – Saturday

Not only is this the best coffee in Downpatrick, in our view, this coffee shop makes great efforts to cross any remaining sectarian divide around here, by displaying the local catholic school's hurling team shirt and the protestant school's rugby shirt.

Tea?

Oakley Fayre Deli

52 Market Street, Downpatrick BT30 6LY

www.oakleyfare.com

Open

Monday – Saturday

This deli in Downpatrick is a mother and son affair: Mum Dolores opened it up over 30 years ago, before son Darren was even born. But he's now trained as a Master Chef so it's well worth popping along here to sample the cakes as well as the excellent Suki Teas...

DROMORE CATHEDRAL OF CHRIST THE REDEEMER

The intimate feel to this cathedral is helped by the pulpit being placed half way along the south wall, rather than at the 'high' end, as in most churches.

Enoch Powell had a specific pew when he was a regular attendee as the local MP; chosen by his security guards, it's NOT in a prominent spot!

Don't miss the 1613 Bible; it's not worth a lot, but there's a lovely story of it being taken to England by an officer after some 17th century battle, and then found 300 years later in a shop in Durham; now returned to Dromore.

The oldest object is probably St Colman's 'pillow', a slab of stone supposedly owned and used as an altar by this local saint when the first church was built on the site in 510AD.

But this church also embraces the future, with its sound deck, room for a band to play, and three fold-down screens for projections during services!

The pews are tightly packed, but face in different directions, largely due to the way the church was built in sections.

Lovely tapestry with a section to show all the towns/churches in the Diocese – why don't all cathedrals have something like this?

No recommended amount for donation; if the church is locked try the office in Church Street.

Coffee?

Olive Branch Coffee Lounge

33 Market Square, Dromore BT25 1AW

www.viawings.co.uk

Open

Daily

What a positive vibe to this coffee shop on Dromore's main street. From the warm welcome you'll get as you enter the place through to the great coffee and home-made scones. And all of it going towards helping the needy of the local community. A great cause.

Tea?

Riverside Tearoom

12 Bridge Street, Dromore, County Down BT25 1AN

Open

Tuesday – Saturday

Great little tea room with views over the River Lagan flowing past and a roaring fire to keep you warm in winter. But best of all are the home-made cakes on offer. What a great find in such a small town.

DUNBLANE CATHEDRAL

There's a memorial to the 1996 shootings in Dunblane: "If there is anything that will endure the eye of God, because it is pure, it is the spirit of a little child".

The roll of honour includes all those from Dunblane who served in the world wars, not just those who gave their lives; and some who fought under the Australian flag, so they had presumably already emigrated Down Under...

The 'Clement Chapel' is the cosiest, most intimate spot in the Cathedral; mediaeval, but only made into a chapel in the 1960s.

The oldest choir stalls date from about 1500, and are those nearest the East window – look for the bat carved into the seat of one stall.

The church bells from the 17th century now sit along the north aisle – look for the engraving of their story carved into each bell.

Recommended donation £2.

Coffee?

Beech Tree Café

2 Beech Road, Dunblane FK15 0AA

Facebook: Beech Tree Cafe

Open

Daily

Best coffee in Dunblane and some wonderful home-baked cakes and scones to choose from. I wonder if Andy Murray used to come down here for a cuppa when he was living here?

Tea?

We found nowhere else we'd like to recommend for tea in Dunblane, so maybe go back to Beech Tree Café for your tea, and have some more cake…

DUNDEE CATHEDRAL – ST PAUL'S
(EPISCOPAL CHURCH)

The stained-glass windows are this cathedral's highlights: don't miss the whale in one of the chancel windows; or Queen Victoria and Prince Albert on their wedding day in one of the south aisle windows.

Look out for the plaque in memory of James Chalmers, the inventor of the adhesive postage stamp – he never patented it, so his name remains unfamiliar to most.

No recommended amount for donation – all 'gratefully received'.

DUNDEE CATHOLIC CATHEDRAL – ST MARY'S

A great feeling of light and space as you enter this cathedral, with the gold-painted wood of the altar dominating the eye.

This is the oldest Catholic church in Dundee, built in 1836.

No mention of donations.

Coffee?

T Ann Cake

27 Exchange Street, Dundee DD1 3DJ

http://t-ann-cake.blogspot.com/
Facebook: T Ann Cake

Open

Tuesday – Saturday

The décor and furniture in this central Dundee coffee shop is a retro-lover's dream. And once you've had one of their home-baked cakes, you won't be surprised to learn that owner Ann has been nominated for awards across Scotland for her baking. Great place for a cuppa.

Tea?

Sadly, our favourite place for tea in Dundee, TLC, closed its doors in June 2013. You'll just have to go back to T Ann Cake and have a pot of their finest, with some more cake…

DUNKELD CATHEDRAL

Possibly the most beautiful setting for a cathedral anywhere: on the banks of the River Tay, this cathedral is half ruin and half parish church these days.

Dunkeld's High Street used to run right alongside and past the Cathedral until virtually the whole town was burnt to the ground in the 1689 Battle of Dunkeld; look out for the holes in the walls and pillars, especially in the ruined sections: yes, these were 1689 bullets and leadshot marks from the same battle.

The Wolf of Badenoch is an impressive figure dating from the 14th century, now laid out behind the altar, looking very knightly.

Dunkeld's curfew bell, rung every night at 8pm and every morning at 6am until the start of the First World War, now sits in the Cathedral's Chapter House.

You're asked to pay £1 for the excellent audio tour on offer, but donations are all voluntary.

Coffee?

Scottish Deli

1 Atholl Street, Dunkeld PH8 0AR

www.scottish-deli.com

Open

Daily

Coffee roasted by a small supplier in the Perthshire highlands, cakes baked by the staff themselves and lots of the produce sold in the deli coming from the owners' own smallholding in nearby Pitlochry. If only you could get this sort of quality on every small town UK High Street.

Tea?

Spill the Beans

6 Cathedral Street, Dunkeld PH8 0AW

Facebook: Spill the Beans @ Macphails of Dunkeld

Open

Daily in summer (check Facebook page for winter)

If 'Good karma makes good cakes' is the motto of this tea room, there must be lots of good karma around the place. Fantastic selection of cakes to go with your pot of tea and all this a short stroll from the Cathedral on what was once Dunkeld's main street.

DURHAM CATHEDRAL

Bill Bryson has apparently called it the 'best cathedral on planet earth'; even King Canute came here to pay homage.

Look out for the fugitives knocker on the main door: any fugitive could enter and receive 37 days of protection before deciding whether to stand trial or take the first ship out of the country.

Anglican Cathedral built between 1093 and 1133 – believed to have the first ever pointed arch vaults in its ceiling and enormous pillars because they didn't know how much weight the pillars needed to bear.

Harry Potter's Hogwarts School of Witchcraft was based here, though they added a computer-generated spire to the 15th century tower.

3,000 Scottish prisoners were held here in 1650 after the Battle of Dunbar – they burnt everything they could find made of wood... except for the astronomical clock, perhaps because of the carved thistle on top?

Look for the Durham Miners' Association banner and the miners' book of remembrance for those who died in the mines.

See St Cuthbert's and the Venerable Bede's tombs, at either end of the Cathedral.

There is no admission charge, but a recommended donation of £5 or pay to have an excellent guided tour and to climb the 325 steps up the tower.

Coffee?

Flat White

21A Elvet Bridge, Durham DH1 3AA

Facebook: Flat-White-Durham

Open

Daily

The two young guys who run Flat White Coffee in Durham will not only make you a great cup of coffee, inspired by their experience in Australia, but they're up bright and early every morning to bake the cakes themselves, too. Oh, and they discovered part of Durham's 13th century city walls when they refurbished the place.

Tea?

Tealicious

88 Elvet Bridge, Durham DH1 3AG

www.tealicioustearoom.co.uk
@TealiciousUK

Open

Tuesday – Saturday

I love the way Durham combines the elegance of the university and cathedral with its history of connections to the coalfields round here. And this tea room mirrors that perfectly, with beautiful décor, freshly-made cakes, and a good strong 'Durham Miner's Brew' – an excellent loose-leaf tea. This is just what Durham needed.

EDINBURGH CATHEDRAL – ST GILES
(PRESBYTERIAN – CHURCH OF SCOTLAND)

If chivalry shivers your timbers, go to the Thistle Chapel, where the 16 Knights of the Thistle meet from time to time. A few days before our visit, Prince William, Duke of Cambridge was formally appointed in the presence of The Queen.

There's a memorial stool, commemorating the moment in 1637 when Jenny Geddes threw her stool in disgust at the new form of worship that was to be introduced and that led to...The National Covenant (on display here). It set up the Church of Scotland, with a severe looking John Knox leading the movement – his image and words are to be seen throughout the Cathedral.

Don't miss the bronze portrait of Robert Louis Stevenson on the west wall – spot the blanket in recognition of his almost constant ill-health through his life.

On a lighter note, and back in the Thistle Chapel, don't miss the carvings of animals in the arm rests of the knights' chairs – elephants, bears, dogs, deer, rams...

Recommended donation of £3.

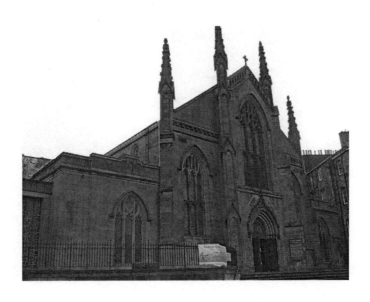

EDINBURGH METROPOLITAN CATHEDRAL – ST MARY'S (CATHOLIC)

The National Shrine to St Andrew is the key feature here, with its eastern orthodox-looking icons. Also contains two jars of relics from St Andrew, one of them looks like a shoulder joint…

No specific amount recommended for donations.

EDINBURGH EPISCOPAL CATHEDRAL – ST MARY'S

The King Charles Chapel has a portrait of Charles I with the inscription: "King Charles, the Martyr"; there's also a copy of the warrant for his execution in 1649.

The 17th century house next door was the home of two sisters who left the land in their will for a cathedral to be built – their photograph is pinned to the wall as you enter at the west door.

The pew belonging to the 'greatest Scot of all times', Sir Walter Scott, is in this cathedral, although Scott died a couple of hundred years before the Cathedral was built.

No specific amount recommended for donations.

Coffee?

Freemans Coffee

2-6 Spottiswoode Road, Edinburgh EH9 1BQ

www.freemanscoffee.co.uk
@freemanscoffee

Open

Daily

This relative newcomer to Edinburgh's coffee scene is well worth the stroll across The Meadows to the Marchmont District. Great coffee from Climpsons in London, Kiwi cookies and tray bakes by Marg, and an overall good feel to this place set up by ex-Army officer David.

More coffee?

Brew Lab Coffee

6-8 South College Street, Edinburgh EH8 9AA

www.brewlabcoffee.co.uk

@BrewLabCoffee

Open

Daily

This is one of a new generation of coffee shops that built up a customer-base on social media months before they actually opened. That way, they knew what customers wanted: it's not just the free wifi and sockets in all the walls; it's also the excellent coffee and cakes; and an overall good atmosphere. I'd be dropping in most days if I lived in Edinburgh.

Tea?

lovecrumbs

155 West Port, Edinburgh EH3 9DP

www.lovecrumbs.co.uk
@hellolovecrumbs

Open

Daily

The two women who run this lovely tea room in Westport started out by baking exotic sponge cakes for local coffee shops. Now they've set up shop themselves in a place that started life as a grocer's in 1845 and have introduced their own quirky style, with tea crates as tables and a wardrobe to display the cakes.

More tea?

Eteaket

41 Frederick Street, Edinburgh EH2 1EP

www.eteaket.co.uk
@eteaket

Open

Daily

You might be carried away by Eteaket's excellent loose-leaf teas and home-made scones. But you'll also be inspired by the story of Eteaket's owner, who turned to tea after suffering serious injuries in a skiing accident. She travelled to China and Sri Lanka to study tea and to meet the people involved, and has turned her life around with this marvellous business.

ELY CATHEDRAL

The octagon tower, with its 'lantern' top is most people's highlight in Ely. Built in 1340, it is unique in the UK. It has 200 tonnes of timber forming the frame. The angels in the lantern part are painted on doors and if you go up that high you can open a door and look out over the city and surrounds.

There was a monastery on the site at first, but the Isle of Ely was surrounded by swamps so treacherous that even William the Conqueror's army didn't manage to take the place; after five years of siege, the monks did show them the path through the marsh, though, and the Saxon church was demolished.

Ely Cathedral can be seen from miles around because of the flat landscape of the Fens; it's said that you can even see it from the top of King's College in Cambridge, some 17 miles away.

There are fantastic Norman arches right along the nave, but there's something rather sinister about the Tabula Eliensis, a painting that depicts Norman knights sitting with the Benedictine monks after the defeat of the Saxons.

The Prior's Door was built in the mid 12th century; don't miss a rare sight of Christ without a beard; and look out for signs of the zodiac on the heavenly side of the door; with images of booze, music and play on the 'worldly' side.

The enormous Lady Chapel was built in the 1340s, though Henry VIII's cronies knocked the heads off nearly all the carved figures in the niches.

Brithnoth was an Earl of Essex who really did lose his head at the Battle of Maldon in AD991. His headless body is buried in Bishop West's Chantry Chapel, with apparently a head-sized ball of hard wax on top of the clavicle…

There's a £7 admission fee and it's even more to go up into the tower; but you do get a free guided tour of the main cathedral for your ticket entrance.

Coffee?

Sadly, the independent coffee shop we knew and liked in Ely closed down during 2012.

Tea?

Peacocks Tearoom

65 Waterside, Ely CB7 4AU

www.peacockstearoom.co.uk

Open

Wednesday – Sunday

If this feels like being invited to someone's home for afternoon tea, that's because the owners do live here and the chances are you'll have your cuppa in the living room or parlour! A fantastic selection of loose-leaf teas from all the continents of the world (except Antarctica...)

ENNISKILLEN CATHEDRAL – ST MACARTIN'S

With two regiments historically based in Enniskillen, this cathedral is full of military memorabilia, with an extraordinary range of worldwide endeavours, beginning in Martinique in 1762. Not everyone died in action, though: one captain died of sunstroke in Burma; another died in Dover on his return from war!

Don't miss the Pokrich Stone, mounted in the west wall. William Pokrich was no pirate, in spite of the skull and crossbones; the inscription on his stone reproduces the final words of Thomas Cromwell, beheaded by Henry VIII in 1540.

The font has been in place here since 1666, though you won't find many babies small enough to be submerged in this water...

Some of the East Window glass had to be replaced after the Enniskillen bombing in 1987.

No recommended amount for donation.

Coffee?

Johnstons Jolly Sandwich Bar

3 Darling Street, Enniskillen BT74 7DP

Facebook: The Jolly Sandwich Bar

Open

Monday – Saturday

If you're on a Cathedral Coffee Tour, you can't do better than this coffee shop right next door to Enniskillen Cathedral. It's a friendly, family-run business, with cakes so good it has made it into the Good Food Guide. Not to be missed for a cuppa in Enniskillen.

Tea?

Frou Frou

37 Townhall Street, Enniskillen BT74 7BD

Facebook: Frou Frou

Open

Daily

The best Victoria Sponge we'd eaten for quite a while. Not surprising when you learn that owner Julie is up half the night baking fresh cakes for Frou Frou and her other two tea rooms in the area. This one gets our vote, though, with its setting in a beautiful old retail outlet on Enniskillen's main street.

EXETER CATHEDRAL

The mediaeval vaulted ceiling runs the full length of the Cathedral, almost 100m in length; said to be the longest continuous mediaeval vault in the world.

> Look at the embroidered cushions that run along the walls, starting mid-way along the south aisle: they trace the history of Exeter and the Cathedral through the centuries.

The Minstrels' Gallery dates from 1360 – it has carved angels playing musical instruments; but a debate is raging around what the missing instrument might be; and why is there no lute here?

> In case you ever had any doubts about the status and grandeur of bishops in mediaeval times, the cathedra in Exeter Cathedral will dispel those immediately.

What's also missing is any reference (that we could see) to Agnes Prest, a protestant martyr who was apparently in the Cathedral when she predicted her own death in 1557 – there is a memorial to her near the city walls, though.

Look at the memorial to those from a local regiment that died in India in 1860: far more were lost through the 'effects of climate' than died in action!

The sledge flag of Robert Scott, the Antarctic explorer, is displayed on the south wall.

Loveliest modern artwork? We'd say the bronze mother nursing a baby by local sculptor, Janis Ridley, in 2006 (opposite the Lady Chapel).

Best bit of trivia? Check out the round hole at the bottom of an old door near the astronomical clock. It is said to have been cut between 1598 and 1621 so that the then Bishop's cat could easily catch mice trying to climb the clock's ropes.

There is a £5 fee to enter this Cathedral.

Coffee?

Devon Coffee

88 Queen Street, Exeter EX4 3RP

Tel: 07795 105 250
@coffeedevon

Open

Daily

Why would anyone choose a corporate coffee place over a great little independent coffee shop like this one in the centre of Exeter? It's not just the quality of the coffee and the choice of beans and roast, it's the friendly, intimate atmosphere and the sense of history here with the bill posters they have uncovered from 1908!

More coffee?

Café at 36

36 Cowick Street, Exeter EX4 1AW

www.cafeat36.co.uk
@CafeAt36

Open

Daily

There's a real sense of community as soon as you walk into this café down near St Thomas Station in Exeter. There are artists, poets, musicians, but also just foot-weary shoppers, not to mention those who come here just because the coffee (and the tea) is excellent.

Tea?

Jolly Roger Tea Room

Waterside, Exeter EX2 8GX

No web presence

Open

Daily

There's a bit of a nautical theme to this tea room, with tea clippers on the wall, yachts berthed outside and a life-sized pirate out the front to welcome people in. But it's the quality of the tea and excellent home-made cakes that made it one of my favourite tea rooms on this tour.

GLASGOW CATHEDRAL –
ST MUNGO'S CHURCH OF SCOTLAND

In 1451 the Pope said a pilgrimage to St Mungo's tomb here was as important as a visit to Rome (the tomb is still there, by the way).

Check out the lion and the unicorn in the Sacristy – they swapped flags, in a sign of reconciliation between England and Scotland.

The window commemorating the Glasgow tradesmen has all the usual trades, but also barbers, woodbinds and cordiners…

There's a 15th century oak door to the Sacristy, with 17th century bullet holes, from earlier times of religious strife…

Don't miss the 1617 Bible on display and make sure you hear the full story of how it was stolen and then returned to the Cathedral.

Look for the little ladybird in the ceremonial chair for the Royal Navy – there's a good luck story from World War Two here too...

Look out for the window dedicated to Robert Louis Stevenson's grandfather, who was in charge of lighthouses round these parts...

The well in the under-church (which is not a crypt because it has windows) leads directly to the burn running below the Cathedral.

No recommended donation but the free guided tours are worth a generous response...

ST ANDREW'S ROMAN CATHOLIC CATHEDRAL

Highlight is actually outside beside the Cathedral. The Italian Cloister Garden has a mirrored labyrinth with biblical quotes to remind us of mortality.

The memorial in the garden is to Italian civilian prisoners who died when the ship SS Arandora Star was torpedoed off the Irish coast in 1940 – the people of Tuscany sent a 200 year-old olive tree, though it seems to be struggling in Glasgow's climate.

The constant trickling of the water in the new font gives the Cathedral a feeling of peace and continuity.

Don't miss the steel sculptures of Scottish saints in one of the chapels – part of the 2012 renovations.

No request for donations, so go for the very good guide for visitors at £1 each.

ST MARY'S EPISCOPAL CATHEDRAL

Has the only peal of bells in the whole of Glasgow!

New York-based artist Gwyneth Leech did most of the murals around the Cathedral, when she lived in the UK in the 1990s.

This has one of those rare memorials to the World War One dead that refers to the dates 1914-1920...

No recommended amount for donations.

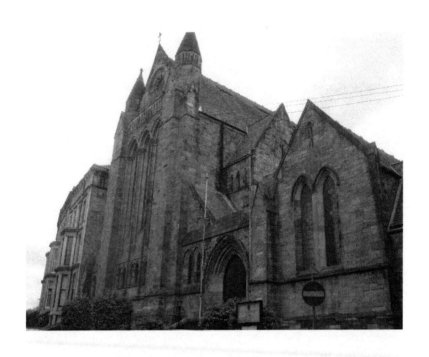

ST LUKE'S GREEK ORTHODOX CATHEDRAL

The Greek community in Glasgow set up their first church in 1944, but received a massive donation in the 1960s allowing them to buy this former Presbyterian church to be their Cathedral in Glasgow.

The building was locked on the day of our visit; and a search suggests that members of the public are only able to visit at Easter or on Glasgow's Doors Open Day (September each year).

Coffee?

Artisan Roast

17 Gibson Street, Glasgow G12 8NU

www.artisanroast.co.uk
@artisanroast

Open

Daily

Quality coffee in what must be one of the nicest streets in Glasgow. They used to roast their own coffee here on-site, but the place became so popular, they moved the roasting regime to Edinburgh, so you now have lots more space to sit and sip your coffee in a very cosy coffee shop. Fantastic cakes still baked on-site, though!

More coffee?

Riverhill Coffee Bar

24 Gordon Street, Glasgow G1 3PU

Facebook: Riverhill Deli and Cafe
@RiverhillCoffee

Open

Monday – Saturday

At last somewhere in the centre of Glasgow for a decent coffee. This place only opened at the start of 2013, but it's certainly filled a gap in the market, with excellent coffee and cakes baked on-site. Whether you're running for a train, doing your shopping or just passing through Glasgow, this is the place to go for a cuppa.

Tea?

The Hidden Lane Tea Room

8 Argyle Court, 1103 Argyle Street, Glasgow G3 8ND

www.thehiddenlanetearoom.blogspot.com

Open

Daily

Vintage décor, mix and match bone china, home-baked cakes and excellent tea supplied by Tchai-Ovna in Glasgow and Suki Tea in Belfast. A great example of the retro-style tea room, and worth a visit just to see this Hidden Lane behind Glasgow's Argyle Street.

More tea?

Tchai-Ovna House of Tea

42 Otago Lane, Glasgow G12 8PB

www.tchaiovna.com
Facebook: Tchai Ovna

Open

Daily from 11am

This tea room down by the River Kelvin may have been inspired by the tea scene in Prague, but the feel inside is more Bedouin. And if you go for the Bedouin Sage Tea and the Uber slice, you can almost imagine yourself in a North African desert rather than the edge of Glasgow's West End.

GLOUCESTER CATHEDRAL – ST PETER'S

The cloister corridors are so magnificent that they filmed Harry Potter scenes in them (but only after they had blacked out the angel's haloes in the stained glass windows).

The great East Window – built in 1350 – is the size of a tennis court. Spot the 'Gloucester Golfer' in that window. More likely he was playing something called 'bandy ball'.

Henry III was crowned here, at the age of 9 – see the window in the South Wall dedicated to him.

William the Conqueror's son is buried here – see the 800 year old painted wooden carving of him.

No admission charge, but a recommended £5 donation. Guided tours are free and available throughout the day.

Coffee?

Hedley's Tea & Coffee House

66 Westgate Street, Gloucester GL1 2NZ

www.gloucestercoffeeshop.co.uk
@gloscoffeeshop

Open

Monday – Saturday

Have a cup of coffee in what was once a 16th century outfitters on Gloucester's main shopping street. They've won an award for the quality of the renovation work done on this building and the old oak beams will probably last for centuries more to come.

Tea?

Folk Museum Tea Rooms

99-103 Westgate Street Gloucester GL1 2PG

museums.food@gloucester.gov.uk

Open

Tuesday – Saturday

We're rather pleased that Gloucester City Council decided to open this tea room at the back of the Folk Museum. The building was the lodging house of one of Gloucester's 16th century bishops, but it's been a museum since 1935 and is quite the most elegant place for a cuppa and cake in Gloucester today.

GUILDFORD CATHEDRAL OF THE HOLY SPIRIT

The architect focused on 'mass, volume and line rather than the elaborate and ornamental', so this is a modern cathedral that may not appeal to lovers of the mediaeval...

Elizabeth R and Philip are two of the Royals who signed bricks for Guildford's 'Buy a Brick' campaign when money was short for building the place after the War. At 2/6 each, you can see them in the entrance by St Ursula's Porch.

Look out for the small brass stag set in the floor – it represents the high point of Stag Hill, where previous monarchs would hunt in mediaeval times.

Not often the local County Council sponsors a cathedral window, but in Guildford they do, and it has lovely purples brightening up the South side of the church.

Love the map of the Guildford diocese parish churches – gives a real sense of the area. Why don't all cathedrals have something like this?

"Donate what you can," says the sign by the collection box, adding that it costs £1.84 a minute to run the Cathedral…

Coffee?

Glutton & Glee

6 Tunsgate, Guildford GU1 3QT

www.gluttonandglee.co.uk
@GluttonandGlee

Open

Daily

Quality coffee (and tea) in this contemporary-feel deli in one of
Guildford's oldest streets. Lovely ambience, so not surprising the
in-house ghost doesn't want to leave the place...

Tea?

Sadly, we didn't find anywhere else we can recommend for tea
in Guildford, so you'll just have to go back to Glutton & Glee to
try their Rare Tea...

HEREFORD CATHEDRAL – ST MARY & ST ETHELBERT

The Mappa Mundi is a mediaeval map of the world dating from around 1300. Costs £6 to visit the separate exhibition near the Cathedral library.

The map you can see for free shows every single CofE church in the Hereford diocese.

Hereford's Royalist sympathies in the Civil War are commemorated in a stained glass window showing Charles II.

Don't miss the mediaeval wall paintings on the south wall to the Lady Chapel.

The Bishop's Throne is made for 3 people, but look out for the smaller chair he uses for less prestigious occasions.

Recommended £5 donation but the daily guided tour is free.

Coffee?

Bean There?

24-25 Church Street, Hereford HR1 2LR

www.beantherecafe.co.uk

Open

Monday – Saturday

Immerse yourself in travel dreams with maps or books from the shop next door, imagine who's been through the doors of this 14th century building so close to Hereford Cathedral, or just sit back and sip the top quality coffee roasted a few miles away in Ross-on-Wye.

Tea?

Antique Tea Shop

5a St Peters Street, Hereford HR1 2LA

Open

Monday – Saturday (also Sunday during summer school holidays)

Tea is in the family veins of Asanga, who runs this place with wife Miffy. His father ran a blending and packaging firm out of Sri Lanka. Now he plays the perfect host, treating regulars as old friends and newbies as new friends! Great afternoon tea, too!

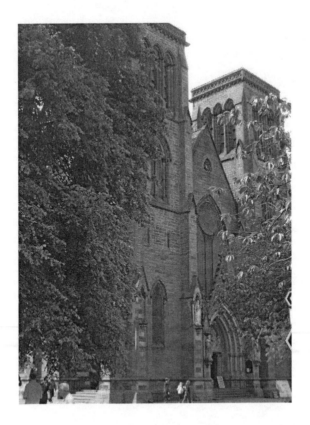

INVERNESS CATHEDRAL – ST ANDREW'S (EPISCOPAL)

One of the few cathedrals built on a North-South axis, so the north-facing 'west window' gets no direct sunlight!

The Russian icons on the wall of the 'north' aisle were a donation from Tsar Alexander II in 1866.

Two paintings on either side of the church as you enter show the Cathedral as it was meant to look, with two tall spires, but they ran out of funds and the spires were never built.

The Bishop's throne is the only surviving piece of original woodwork from when the church was built in the 1860s.

Recommended donation of £3.

Coffee?

The Riverdale Centre

105-107 Church Street, Inverness IV1 1EY

www.therapies-inverness.co.uk

Open

Monday – Saturday

Is this the most relaxing venue in the *Fancy a Cuppa* catalogue? With massage and qi gong, healing and reiki on offer before you have your cuppa and cake, you're bound to leave this place feeling good. And if you sample the home-baked cakes, you'll be on Cloud 9.

Tea?

Leakey's Book Shop & Café

Church Street, Inverness IV1 1EY

Facebook: Leakey's Bookshop & Café

Open

Monday – Saturday

Our idea of heaven: the country's biggest second hand bookshop in a wonderful old church building AND they have a tea room upstairs where you can get a pot of tea and some home-baked cake. If you're like us, you'll find it impossible to leave here without a book or a map under your arm…

KIRKWALL CATHEDRAL – ST MAGNUS

Skulls & crossbones all over the place in this cathedral. Most of the standing headstones around the walls have graphic symbols of death carved into them.

Robert Nicolsone's memorial looks more like a grim pub sign, with a ghostly-looking figure, an egg timer and the bell that tolls. Such signs were common in the 17th century, hung outside the home of someone who had just died, prior to their body being transferred to a holier place.

The bones of St Magnus were found some years ago inside one of the cathedral pillars (the skull was broken in the place the axe would have fallen when he was executed in 1115) – they're back in the same pillar now.

There's a dungeon under this cathedral, where suspected witches apparently used to be held.

Look out for the white, sail-like tapestry, sent to Kirkwall by the town of Hordaland in Norway to mark the 850th anniversary of the Cathedral's founding.

The Cathedral used to host the weekly market in Kirkwall, and during the Civil War and the Commonwealth, it was used for stabling...

This is the only cathedral with three bells, all of which can be rung by the same person simultaneously.

Recommended donation £2.

Coffee?

CafeLolz@21

21 Albert Street, Kirkwall KW15 1HP

Facebook: CafeLolz

Open

Daily

Coffee in Kirkwall is a real family affair, with Lol fixing the coffee and doing most of the baking along with her Mum. Even her Dad gets involved with the washing-up. Best coffee in Kirkwall, and fantastic cakes to go with it.

Tea?

The Strynd Tea Room

Strynd, Kirkwall KW15 1HG

Facebook: The Strynd Tea Room

Open

Monday – Saturday

They reckon this thick stone-walled house might once have been the Kirkwall Castle garden keeper's home. It's a lovely setting now for a traditional afternoon tea on a tiered cake stand. Don't miss the narrow alleyway tucked away off Kirkwall's main street: that's Strynd…

LANCASTER CATHEDRAL – ST PETER'S (CATHOLIC)

Catholic Cathedral – neo-Gothic built in the 1850s, with 240ft high spire.

Look for the Lancashire red roses in the rose window in the south wall.

A piece of Thomas More's hair shirt is kept in the niche of the Thomas More Chapel.

See the statue of St Peter looming above you as you enter; a replica of the St Peter in Rome Basilica, it is carved in wood, except for his right foot…

We liked the windows of King Herod and of Jesus, next to the Baptistry.

Worth picking up a guide to the Cathedral for £2 as you enter; but otherwise a donations box with a choice of slots for your money: church, candles, etc.

Coffee?

Music Room Café

Sun Square, Sun Street, Lancaster LA1 1EW

www.themusicroomcafe.com
Twitter: @coffeehopper

Open

Daily

Award-winning coffee roasted round the corner in a shop that's been in Lancaster for over 175 years. This coffee shop is in a beautiful Georgian building that was once a private residence with bowling green out the front and Greek muses painted on the walls upstairs: that's why it's called the Music Room...

Tea?

Novel Café Books & Coffee Shop

18 New Road, Lancaster LA1 1EG

Across the road from the former Lancaster & Skerton Equitable Co-operative Building

Open

Daily

Best-value cream tea you'll find for miles around and the kind of place where you can sit back and read a book for a few hours while you sip on your tea and scones. They don't want publicity at this café though – just word-of-mouth – so don't tell them where you heard about them...

LEEDS CATHEDRAL – ST ANNE'S (CATHOLIC)

The skulls of two Yorkshire martyrs who were beheaded in York in 1598 lie within the altar of the Cathedral.

Look out for the Yorkshire saints depicted in the Sanctuary.

There are 2,800 pipes within the two organs in the Cathedral – you can sponsor a pipe if you want to donate to the church.

Otherwise, there is no collection box or admission charge and this feels like a fully functional church rather than a tourist attraction: lots of people attending services or confessionals during our visits.

Coffee?

Laynes Espresso

16 New Station Street, Leeds LS1 5DL

www.laynesespresso.co.uk - @laynesespresso

Open

Daily

Owner Dave's favourite football team – Leeds United – may not have made the Premier League yet, but his coffee shop is certainly among the best in the land. This is what they call a 'destination coffee shop' and not just because it's right by Leeds railway station. Coffee is superb, and the ginger cake not to be missed.

Tea?

The Tiled Hall Cafe

Leeds Art Gallery, The Headrow, Leeds LS1 3AA

http://www.boutique-catering.co.uk/

Open

Daily

This cafe is one of the treasures of 19th century Yorkshire, hidden from the public for 50 years until 2007. It was feared that the tiled walls were so beautiful that people would be distracted from reading in what was formerly the library. Now you can enjoy a cuppa while admiring the views.

LEICESTER CATHEDRAL – ST MARTIN'S

They sprinkle white roses over Richard III's tomb in the Cathedral every August to commemorate the battle nearby where he lost his life. His actual remains were rediscovered under a local car park in 2012, though it took until 2013 to prove that the bones really were Richard's. The plan is to bury him in the Cathedral (but this had not taken place as we went to print, and there was some opposition to this from Yorkshire, the White Rose county…).

If you think the figure of St Martin – in the West Window – looks more Roman than British, you'd be right. He was a 4th century Roman Army officer.

Note Joan of Arc appears in the East Window, which commemorates WW1. Her connection to 1914-18? Her link to the town of Ypres…

Don't miss the mediaeval oak chest by the Vaughan entrance. It presumably had three owners because there are three keyholes and once upon a time all the owners would have to be present to open it.

These days, the oak chest is the donations box for the Cathedral. No admission charge, but a recommended £4 donation.

Coffee?

St Martin's Tea & Coffee

Silver Walk, Leicester LE1 5EW

www.stmartinscoffee.co.uk
@StMartinsCoffee

Open

Daily

They roast their own coffee here so the smell may draw you in before you even spot this little coffee shop behind an old staging post in Leicester's city centre. Great quality coffee, and interesting cakes brought to you by a local patissier.

Tea?

Mrs Bridges Tea Rooms

17 Loseby Lane, Leicester LE1 5DR

Facebook: Mrs Bridges Tearooms

Open

Daily

There's been a tea room in this building since 1890. The current owners have stopped using the old ovens in the basement, which is a shame, but perhaps they weren't producing the quality desired by pastry chef Christian, who's in charge of the place these days and makes sure your Afternoon Tea tastes as good as it looks.

LICHFIELD CATHEDRAL OF ST CHAD & ST MARY

The only mediaeval cathedral in England with three spires.

A sniper used one of the three spires during the Civil War to shoot a Royalist standing in the main street 100 yards away – that spire was destroyed during the Civil War's three sieges of Lichfield.

The St Chad Gospels date from the 8th century – all hand-written, they are displayed in the Chapter House.

Don't miss the stairs up to St Chad's Head Chapel, where St Chad's bones were kept until the 1540s, and his skull was exhibited from the balcony overlooking the nave.

Look for the sword marks across the faces of some of the carvings in the north wall – scars left over from civil war battles.

The Lichfield Angel stone, also in the Chapter House, comes from the early Saxon church and is reckoned to be 7th century.

Beautiful floor tiling in the presbytery, but interesting selection of monarchs depicted: Offa, King of Mercia in the late 8th century; Queen Victoria; and King Charles I...

Check out the mediaeval wall paintings: the biggest in the south wall, but also in the Chapter House and South Quire Aisle – lovely reds and yellows.

No admission charge, but strong encouragement to leave a donation.

The venues

Coffee?

The Tudor of Lichfield

Lichfield House, 32 Bore Street, Lichfield WS13 6LL

rest@tudor-lichfield.co.uk
Facebook: The Tudor of Lichfield

Open

Daily

Who can resist having a cuppa in this 500 year old building, with armour in one corner, tapestry hanging on one wall and old Tudor beams outside and in? This place has been owned by the same family since Wilfred and Evelyn Burns-Mace opened it in 1935 – you might even get to meet the current Mr Burns-Mace!

Tea?

Sadly our favourite tea room in Lichfield was a victim of the recession in 2012. We found nowhere else we'd like to recommend, so maybe go back to Tudor of Lichfield for your tea?

LINCOLN CATHEDRAL

There's been a cathedral here since 1092 though most of the current building dates from the 13th and 14th centuries; the original church was said to have been destroyed in an earthquake in 1185...

The railing marking the front of the Sanctuary runs exactly along the path of the Roman wall of the city.

One of the chandeliers is made from metal taken from old Lancaster bombers, in recognition of the number of RAF bases near Lincoln and associated lives lost.

Filming of Dan Brown's "The Da Vinci Code" took place in Lincoln Cathedral.

Lincoln's equivalent of 'Big Ben' is called 'Great Tom' but his vibrations mean he is rarely rung these days.

Don't miss the imp. The one that got into the Cathedral and became the symbol of Lincoln.

Look out for the 32 Green Men – pagan symbols – around the Cathedral; not to mention the many men in green in the stained glass windows – presumably Lincoln Green, as worn by Robin Hood...

There's an admission charge of £6 but you are then entitled to take one of the excellent and free guided tours – 11am & 2pm the day we were there.

Coffee?

Coffee Aroma

24 Guildhall Street, Lincoln LN1 1TR

www.coffeearoma.co.uk
Twitter: @coffee_aroma

Open

Daily

An award-winning barista serving award-winning coffee in a cosy little coffee shop with oak beams that have been there for hundreds of years. These guys may have been featured in the national media, but it hasn't gone to their heads and this was one of the friendliest coffee shops on our cathedral tour.

Tea?

Pimento Tea Rooms

26/27 Steep Hill, Lincoln LN2 1LU

Facebook: Pimento Tearooms

Open

Daily

A tea room in a 900 year old building with views looking up and down Steep Hill in Lincoln. But it's not just the building and the scenery which drew us in: they serve fantastic quality teas, blended just across the road by an old family-run tea business. And the Lincolnshire Plum Bread is pretty good, too!

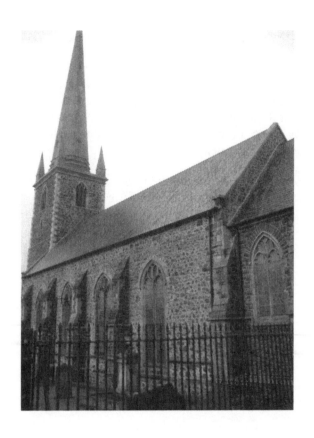

LISBURN CHRIST CHURCH CATHEDRAL

2012 saw a major refurbishment of this cathedral. When it re-opened in December, it had a coffee shop (yes, free cappuccino if you go to Sunday service), fully-equipped sound system; big screens – this is the 21st century after all!

The first cathedral on this site was destroyed in the so-called Rebellion of 1641; only the tower remains today from the 2nd cathedral that was burnt down, along with the rest of Lisburn in the Great Fire of 1707.

1918-1920 were turbulent times for Lisburn Cathedral: suffragettes tried to bomb the east wall in 1918; and one of the IRA's early targets in 1920 was a policeman called Swanzy, who was shot as he left a service at the Cathedral.

Lt Dobbs was a naval leader, most famous for intercepting one of the raids from John Paul Jones (an American ship's captain who was known to sail into British harbours, striking fear into locals during the War of Independence) – but no mention of this incident on his memorial plaque!

No indication of recommended amounts for donation. Buy a cappuccino, at least, if you visit in future…

Coffee?

Sadly, our favourite coffee shop in Lisburn, Molly's Parlour, closed its doors in April 2013, with a move to Belfast on the cards. You'll just have to try the coffee at our recommended venue for tea in Lisburn...

Tea?

Shannon's Coffee Dock

2-4 Market Square, Lisburn BT28 1XB

www.shannonsjewellers.com
@shannonslisburn

Open

Monday – Saturday

There's lots of history to this place: family history in the jewellery business that houses the café and gives it such an elegant entrance; social history, with the building itself having possibly been home to Huguenot refugees in the 18th century; and now making history as the best place in Lisburn for a pot of tea!

LISMORE CATHEDRAL CHURCH OF ST MOLUAG

Three families have connections going right back to the foundation of this cathedral and are still in the congregation today. The Blacks, the Carmichaels and the Livingstones, with the present-day Livingstones still custodians of the original pastoral staff.

The former Bishop's residence is quite a walk away from the Cathedral over hills and fields; it's now a ruined castle.

A quick wander round the old graveyard and a peek at the memorials to those who served in the world wars shows also just how many people come from those three big families, though there are a few others too!

The current church is turned the other way round from the original Cathedral (i.e. the pulpit is at the west end); the door behind the pulpit would once have led to the nave of the original building (now it's a field of thistles and cattle troughs).

Climb the stairs up to a gallery for a view down the church and for close inspection of stained glass windows of St Moluag and St Columba.

No recommended amount for donation.

Tea or coffee?

Isle of Lismore Café

Isle of Lismore, By Oban, Argyll PA34 5UL

www.isleoflismore.com
@lismorecafe

Open

Daily – April to October

Friday – Saturday in March

Sit out on the verandah and drink in the views of rolling hills and grazing sheep. You really wouldn't expect such a quality cuppa in an isolated location like this. And there's home-baked cake every day, with fruit grown on the island when in season.

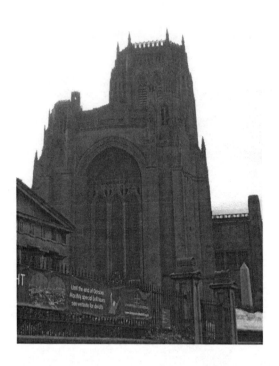

LIVERPOOL CATHEDRAL (ANGLICAN)

This is Britain's biggest cathedral, and the 5th largest in the world.

The Bishop's throne is immovable, as it's carved into the stone of the building; as is the reredos under the east window carved from the original wall.

Have a good look at the Lady Chapel, with its Noble Women windows, including a very pretty young Queen Victoria; and look out for the angel with the football rattle looking down on proceedings here.

There's a memorial to David Sheppard, who was Bishop here in the 1970s, but no mention that he also captained England at cricket a few years earlier…

The carving of the Titanic in the woodwork of the north aisle dates from the 1920s, as does the window dedicated to the Titanic's captain, who lived in Liverpool for some years.

George Melly's brother has a memorial here for his work in Abyssinia, setting up a hospital there until his death in 1936.

Look out for references to the 2nd Bishop of Liverpool: he was a hunchback but two of his sons became Olympic runners.

Recommended donation of £3.

LIVERPOOL METROPOLITAN CATHEDRAL
(CATHOLIC)

The only circular cathedral in the country; built in concrete, it is the ultimate in 'modern' architecture.

Formby Beach meets the Sea of Galilee in one of the larger tapestries; it's woven entirely from recycled material, so the sand bushes, for example, are made from old bin bags!

Blue is the dominant colour inside, especially the vertical windows round the side; but the windows in the tower include all the colours of the spectrum.

The Golden Book of Names includes all those who contributed anything to financing the building of the Cathedral.

The crypt, designed by Lutyens, was all that was built in the 1930s before they ran out of cash and then came up with a completely new design for the Cathedral in the 1960s.

Recommended donation of £3.

Coffee?

Bold Street Coffee

89 Bold Street, Liverpool L1 4HF

www.boldstreetcoffee.co.uk
@boldstcoffee

Open

Daily

Great quality Has Bean coffee and local home-baked cakes make Bold Street Coffee the pick of the places for a cuppa on Liverpool's bohemian Bold Street. And if you're into cycling, you'll find a few fellow travellers in here for sure.

More coffee?

Duke Street Espresso Bar

27 Duke Street, Liverpool L1 5AP

www.dukestespresso.com
@dukestespresso
Facebook: dukestespresso

Open

Daily

'Sister' coffee shop to Bold Street Coffee, Duke Street has that extra bit of design funkiness with its fabulous coffee cup installation strung out across the ceiling. Other than that, the same top quality as you'll find at Bold Street Coffee.

Tea?

LEAF on Bold St

65-67 Bold Street, Liverpool L1 4EZ

www.thisisleaf.co.uk
@leafteashop

Open

Daily

One of our favourite contemporary tea rooms from the first *Fancy a Cuppa?* book, LEAF has gone one step better by moving to this wonderful building in Bold Street, which used to be a tea room in the 1920s. Same quality cuppa as before, though, so we'll keep coming back.

ST PAUL'S CATHEDRAL – CITY OF LONDON

Nobody was whispering during our visit to the Whispering Gallery, 257 steps up from the floor of the Cathedral, but it's worth the climb just to be closer to the ceiling paintings under the famous dome (total 396 steps up to the Stone Gallery for views all over London + another 132 steps to the Golden Gallery, 85m up).

The South West Tower has a bell bigger than Big Ben and a spiral staircase that has film-makers rushing to use; Harry Potter and Madness of King George filmed here; can't believe Hitchcock didn't…

Henry Moore himself chose the spot for his mother and child sculpture, which tells three stories, depending on the angle you look at it from.

Look at the scorch marks on the urn carrying the sculpture of poet John Donne: the Great Fire of London left its mark.

The 27ft high great west doors have the original mediaeval lock still attached to them; they're only opened for visits from The Queen, archbishops or the Lord Mayor of London (no, not Boris or Ken…).

In the crypt are the tombs of many famous figures. Our favourite is William Russell, the first war correspondent who used telegraphs to send back dispatches from the Crimea – his articles apparently inspired Florence Nightingale in to action…

Music lovers may also like the grave of Mr Sullivan, though I wonder how it feels to be kept apart from Mr Gilbert (whose ashes are buried away in north London); also for those who sing 'Jerusalem' regularly, there's Blake (words) and Parry (music) down in the crypt, too.

The chapel to the American Dead of World War II has stained glass windows showing the flags or crests of all the US states.

There's no escaping the £15 entrance fee here, though there is at least a side chapel open for private prayer for those who want to use the building for its original purpose rather than be treated as tourists. Fee includes free guided tour (human or audio).

Coffee?

Workshop Coffee

27 Clerkenwell Road, London EC1M 5RN

http://www.workshopcoffee.com/
@WorkshopCoffee

Open

Daily

Small-batch roasting on-site, cakes baked upstairs, and a décor that combines a night-club feel (because this used to be a night club) with an architect's fantasy (vertical gardens up an inside wall). This place is very special. Fantastic coffee, and open every day.

More coffee?

Association Coffee

10-12 Creechurch Lane, London EC3A 5AY

http://www.associationcoffee.com/
@AssociationEC3

Open

Monday – Friday

These guys have their coffee-making down to a fine art: they use beans from fantastic roasters (Workshop & Square Mile); each brew is stop-watch timed to perfection; and a great system in place even when busy. Love the historical connections to the old tea & coffee warehouse, too.

Tea?

Bea's of Bloomsbury

83 Watling Street, London EC4M 9BX

http://www.beasofbloomsbury.com/
@beas_bloomsbury

Open

Daily

Afternoon tea within sight of St Paul's Cathedral, and a quality pot of tea at that. This place oozes contemporary style, but with a nod to tradition as all the cakes are served on tiered platters.

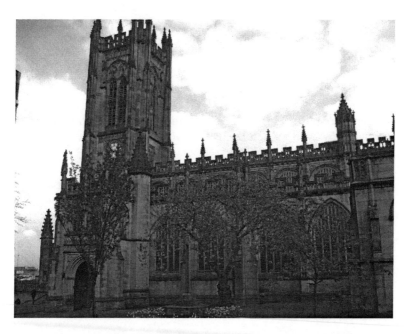

MANCHESTER CATHEDRAL OF SAINT GEORGE, SAINT MARY AND SAINT DENYS

The oldest part of the Cathedral is 14th century, but much of what you see is Victorian, with one whole section rebuilt after Luftwaffe bombing in 1940, and a tiny section damaged in the 1996 IRA bombing.

Look out for kangaroos carved into the Bishop's throne; the 3rd Bishop of Manchester had previously been Bishop of Melbourne in Australia.

WW1 poet Wilfred Owen was in the Manchester Regiment – there's a plaque in his name in the Regiment Chapel.

There are 'Derbyshire Squiggles' all over the floor; fossils embedded in the stone flooring which has been there since the Cathedral was built in mediaeval days.

The 'Angel Orchestra' has golden instruments (wind on north side; strings on south side) from the mediaeval period looking down over the nave.

Look out for the 8th century 'Angel Stone' found nearby and presumed to be from a Saxon church on the site.

During the Civil War, parliamentary snipers defended Manchester from the roof of the Cathedral.

There are photos of the Cathedral in the days after the Luftwaffe attacks in 1940, which destroyed all the mediaeval stained glass windows.

Fantastic colours in the modern stained glass windows in both the west windows and the Fire Window, which commemorates the WW2 bombings.

No admission charge and no suggested amount.

Coffee?

North Tea Power

36 Tib Street, Manchester M4 1LA

www.northteapower.co.uk
Twitter: @northteapower

Open

Daily

This place opened as a tea specialist, but their coffee skills have developed to such an extent that they were voted best coffee shop in Manchester's 2012 Food and Drink Awards. For a while they were the only place in central Manchester to get a top quality coffee, and they're in the super bohemian, arty Northern Quarter – coffee in style!

More coffee?

Caffeine and Co

11 St James's Square, Manchester M2 6WE

@caffeineandco

Open

Monday – Saturday

These are the new kids on the block in Manchester's coffee scene and with the wonderful Square Mile coffee from London, it'll be hard to draw yourself away. But they're not open on Sunday so then you'll just have to hang out in the Northern Quarter…

Tea?

Teacup on Thomas Street

53 Thomas Street, Manchester M4 1NA

www.teacupandcakes.com
Twitter: @teacupandcakes

Open

Daily

Teacup is owned by a local DJ who has been on the music scene around Manchester since the 1980s. He has always liked a good brew and still serves tea at the back of his gigs. Now he has his own tea company, and this place – in the heart of Manchester's Northern Quarter – does a slap up afternoon tea with great cakes.

Afternoon tea?

Richmond Tea Rooms

Richmond Street, Manchester M1 3HZ

www.richmondtearooms.com
Twitter: @Richmond_Tea_Rooms

Open

Daily

Décor inspired by Tim Burton? Chintz and chandeliers? Velvet curtains and vintage records? Yes, this tea room may well be on the edge of Manchester's gay Village, but actually its clientele comes from a much wider community and at 4pm in the afternoon you may have to wait for a table!

MIDDLESBROUGH CATHEDRAL – ST MARY'S

Roman Catholic Cathedral, built in the 1980s, so one of the UK's newest cathedrals (replacing the old town centre cathedral, which burnt down in 2000).

> Beautiful abstract art behind the altar – go to the website www.middlesbroughcathedral.org to find out what it's all about!

Collection tray very discreetly asks for donations to nominated Catholic charities.

> Cathedral placed in one of Middlesbrough's southern suburbs, a half hour bus ride from town (number 11) – nearer the people they serve apparently...

Coffee?

Bahia Cappuccino Bar & Bistro

300 Linthorpe Road, Middlesbrough TS1 3QU

Open

Monday – Saturday

Owner Eduardo de Melo has brought the world to Middlesbrough, with his Italian/Brazilian coffee, photos of Che Guevara on the walls, and global music playing all day. It's the best coffee we found in Middlesbrough!

Tea?

Olde Young Tea House

84 Grange Road, Middlesbrough TS1 2LS

www.oldeyoungteahouse.com – @OldeYoungTHouse

Open

Monday – Saturday

There are 60 different loose-leaf teas to choose from in this cosy little vintage tea room run by fashion enterprise graduate Carli, who now bakes the daily cake herself as well as running the tea room. Love the old advertising on the walls and the old oak counter, which comes from a Salford haberdasher!

CATHEDRAL OF THE ISLES, MILLPORT – CUMBRAE

With room for only 80 at a service in the nave, this is the smallest cathedral in Britain.

The West Window was apparently blown in by a storm during evensong in December 1879, the same night the wind blew down the Tay Rail Bridge.

First time we had seen a sign warning that you need to keep the door closed – to prevent swallows flying in and getting trapped!

How many pianos and other keyboard instruments can you fit into such a small church?

Don't miss the Celtic crosses and other remains from early Christianity on the island – just to your left as you enter.

There is a cross near the Lady Chapel donated by St John the Divine in New York.

No recommended amount for donation…

Coffee?

The Dancing Midge Café

24 Glasgow Street, Millport, Isle of Cumbrae

www.thedancingmidgecafe.com

Open

Daily (mid-March to mid-October only)

If you're lucky you'll get a sighting of seals or dolphins as you sip your cuppa in this café that sits on the sea front, looking out over the Firth of Clyde. Beware, though: only open from March to October...

Tea?

Fintry Bay Tea Rooms

Isle of Cumbrae KA28 0HA

http://millport.org/place/fintry-bay-tearoom/

Open

Daily (Easter to October only)

This is the place to go if you're walking or cycling round the Isle of Cumbrae and fancy a cuppa half way round. Superb views out to sea and a nice pot of tea to refuel before you continue the trip round the island.

MOTHERWELL CATHEDRAL
– OUR LADY OF GOOD AID

Catholic Cathedral built 1899 in the local red sandstone.

Shrine to St John Ogilvie, who was martyred in Glasgow in 1615 – life-sized wood-carved sculpture brought in during the 1980s renovation.

No admission charge and just four simple wooden boxes for collection for: St Anthony, Holy Souls, MacMillan Nurses, Third World.

Coffee?

Kuppas Hardback Café

Motherwell Library, 31 Hamilton Road, Motherwell ML1 3BZ

http://www.northlanarkshire.gov.uk/index.aspx?articleid=6149

Open

Monday – Friday

Best coffee in Motherwell? We'd have no hesitation in recommending this local authority-run café in the town's central library. And if you have a shortbread to go with it, that's been made by the local school dinners service, so you can see how lucky the kids are round here!

Tea?

Scoffs Coffee House

12-14 Muir Street, Motherwell ML1 1BN

Open

Monday – Saturday

One of those places that calls itself a coffee house, but we preferred it for tea and home-made scones. Scoffs is run by another pair of sisters; if they're not twins, they certainly look similar enough for us to do a double-take when they appeared through different doors at the same time...

NEWCASTLE CATHEDRAL – ST NICHOLAS

The 1448 spire was a navigation point for ships on the Tyne.

Church of England, a cathedral since 1882; a parish church since the 13th century.

See the piece of wood from the Roman bridge over the Tyne, built around the time Christ was born.

Look for the effigy of the Unknown Knight (probably served under Edward I between 1272 and 1307).

The 15th century font was hidden from marauding Scots in 1640.

A Danish memorial remembers Danish sailors who used Newcastle as their home from 1940-45.

Lift the canons' seats in the choir for wonderful carvings.

Memorial to Cuthbert Collingwood, the Admiral who finished the Battle of Trafalgar after Nelson's death.

No pressure to donate so don't miss the collection box on the way out.

NEWCASTLE ST MARY'S CATHEDRAL (CATHOLIC)

Built between 1842 and 1844, with a crypt which had to be sealed up by 1848 after a bishop and a priest died of cholera and were then buried there. It's now reopened...

Some of the new and remaining windows are fantastic: the Great East window, designed by the original architect Pugin; and the most recent addition: the 2006 industrial scenes with flat-capped miners, shipbuilders and others.

At the time of our visit no leaflets and little info around the church, so best study the website in advance of any visit: www.stmaryscathedral.org.uk.

Coffee?

Flat Caps Coffee

13 Ridley Place, Newcastle-upon-Tyne, Tyne and Wear NE1 8JQ

www.flatcapscoffee.com
@flatcapjoes

Open

Monday – Saturday

Award-winning coffee shop with a top barista who likes to try new things for UK National Barista Championships. This cosy little coffee shop is tucked away under an exotic arty gift shop just off one of Newcastle's main shopping streets. Coffee roasted locally at Pumphrey's.

More coffee?

Pumphrey's

Grainger Market – opposite Sarah's Tuck-In, and round the corner from Marks & Spencer's Penny Bazaar,

Newcastle-upon-Tyne NE1 5QG

www.pumphreys-coffee.co.uk
@PumphreysCoffee

Open

Monday – Friday

Pumphrey's started life as a tea merchants in Newcastle's Flesh Market in the 1750s, but they've been roasting coffee in town for some time now and some say they 'brought coffee to the north'! This espresso bar in the beautiful Grainger Market has been up and running since October 2011.

Tea?

Tea Sutra

1st Floor, 2 Leazes Park Road, Newcastle upon Tyne, NE1 4PF

www.teasutra.co.uk - @teasutra

Open

Monday – Saturday

There are more than 100 teas to choose from in this tea room modelled on similar places in Barcelona and Prague. Tea Sutra brands itself as: The North East's biggest tea happening since Earl Grey took a fancy to Bergamot. Run by two Buddhist guys, but there's no pressure to take off your shoes or sit on oriental mats. Just enjoy a great cuppa in a relaxing setting.

And for Afternoon Tea?

Jesmond Dene House

Jesmond Dene Road, Newcastle Upon Tyne, Tyne And Wear NE2 2EY

www.jesmonddenehouse.co.uk

Open

Afternoon Tea served 3.00pm – 4.30pm Monday – Saturday; 3.30pm – 5.00pm Sunday

A perfect afternoon in Newcastle involves a walk up the beautiful Jesmond Dene Valley before afternoon tea at this hotel, which used to be the family home of physicist Sir Andrew Noble. Tea is served in a beautiful oak-panelled room with sandwiches and scones presented on an elegant tiered platter with a pot of locally-blended Rington's Tea.

NEWPORT CATHEDRAL – ST WOOLOS (GWYNLLYW)

20 Chartists are buried in Newport Cathedral. These were the guys who were killed while protesting for the right to vote in 1839.

The first church on this site was built in 520AD, after Gwynllyw saw a white ox with a black spot on the forehead (as he had seen in a dream…).

The leper window is now high above the ground but once upon a time this was the only way lepers could see the altar – from outside of course…

The guy in charge round here is called the Bishop of Monmouth rather than the Bishop of Newport, but there is no cathedral in Monmouth.

Gwynllyw's daughter Maches and his wife Gwladus were beautiful women if the Victorian stained glass windows are accurate.

Look out for the tell-tale mouse carved into the choir stalls – the signature of carpenter Robert Thompson…

A very modest donation box in the wall of the Cathedral. Very easy to miss so make sure you donate: this cathedral has a great sense of peace about it.

Coffee?

Java Coffee House

1 Charles Street, Newport NP20 1JU

Open

Monday – Saturday

When local couple Alun and Helen took on this place a few years ago, the first thing they did was to change to a top quality coffee supplier and they increased the number of cakes they baked themselves. Combine quality coffee, home-baking and their excellent approach to customer service and you have the best place for coffee in Newport.

Tea?

Sadly, we didn't find anywhere we can recommend for tea in Newport.

NEWRY (RC) CATHEDRAL (ST PATRICK & ST COLMAN)

Built in 1829, this was the first Catholic cathedral to be built after the Catholic Emancipation Act – in fact it was almost certainly completed just BEFORE it was legal to do so!

> The story goes that the architect was working on Dundalk Cathedral at the same time, and got his plans mixed up, sending his Newry workmen the Dundalk plans – we didn't get over the border to Dundalk to check how similar the two are…

Beautiful mosaic covers the floor and the walls from floor to ceiling; they brought Italians in to do the work, which took five years to complete.

No recommended amount for donation.

Coffee?

Grounded Espresso

10 Merchants Quay, Newry BT35 6AH

www.groundedespresso.com
Facebook: groundedespressobars
@groundedebars

Open

Daily

This place is all about community, whether local or global. There are messages all over the walls, and they serve seriously good coffee. But before you start thinking it's all a bit earnest, check out the cheesy one-liners on the cups and napkins and wait till you arrive to experience the banter from the baristas...

Tea?

Sadly, we didn't find anywhere else we can recommend for tea in Newry, so you'll just have to go back to Grounded to try their loose-leaf tea...

NORTHAMPTON CATHEDRAL
– ST ANDREW'S (CATHOLIC)

Best vantage point for viewing this cathedral is up in the choir gallery by the west window.

You can see St Crispin (patron saint of shoemakers) in one of the west windows, wearing snazzy blue boots in one window, and bashing a few soles in another...

Caroline Chisholm is not buried in the Cathedral grounds but she was a local lass who went to Australia in the 1830s and helped women and children who emigrated there. She returned home in the 1870s and her funeral was in this cathedral (buried a mile away, though) – later recognised on the Australian $5 note!

Thomas a Beckett stands against the south wall; a sword rather graphically cuts right through his head; if this weren't in a holy place, you might think it looks like a circus act.

No recommended amount for donation.

Coffee?

Caffe d'Italia

5 Fish Street, Northampton NN1 2AA

Open

Daily

This little bit of Italy in the heart of Northampton was appreciated even by Russell Crowe who dropped by for a coffee during the filming of Les Misérables round here. It's certainly our choice for coffee in Northampton.

Tea?

Are You Being Served?

62 St Giles Street, Northampton NN1 1JW

@aybsnorthampton

Open

Monday – Saturday

Lovely loose-leaf tea blended just up the road and delicious cakes made by owners Wendy and Chris. These two used to be local teachers and their current class of customers includes the local Northampton rugby team who drop by regularly for some healthy green tea!

NORWICH CATHEDRAL

A lightning strike in 1463 put paid to the old roof and part of the interior; quite nice stone vaulting replaced it afterwards.

Look out for Thomas Gooding's vertical grave in the south wall. There's an eery poem carved into his memorial stone… "As you are now, even so was I; and as I am now so shall you be…"

Norwich City football players are carved into two of the misericordiae – I don't think they date from mediaeval times…

The grandfather and great-grandfather of Ann Boleyn ensured that the family crest would appear in this cathedral.

Don't miss the mediaeval wall paintings, especially in the Jesus

Chapel, where you can spot a picture of Norwich Cathedral as it looked without its spire before that lightning strike.

Into the cloister, you'll have to look hard to spot the small holes for marbles to fit for the monks who wanted to play board games, rather than worship all the time!

Donation of £5 recommended – free guided tours are excellent.

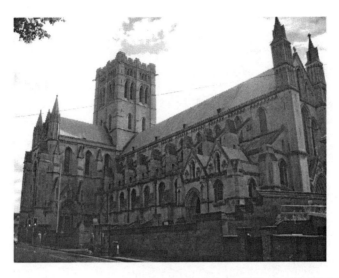

CATHEDRAL OF ST JOHN THE BAPTIST (CATHOLIC)

It's an 'eco-Cathedral', with biomass heating systems. The smoke now passes up through the west pinnacle, so don't call the fire brigade out, as one local resident did when they first saw it.

Check the photo exhibition in the narthex: see how close a bomb came to hitting the Cathedral in 1942; and see the double-decker bus that tipped into an old chalk or flint mine shaft a few years back – hope there's nothing similar under the church itself...

This is the 2nd biggest Catholic cathedral in the UK (after Westminster).

They claim the best views of Norwich are from the Cathedral tower (tours on Saturdays in summer); the tower was also used as a turning point for bomber pilots returning from raids in World War 2.

There's a portrait on the north wall dedicated to Polish armed servicemen who lost their lives in WW2; the painting was blessed by Pope John Paul II during his visit in 1982.

No recommended amount for donations, but they need money for a new lighting system.

Coffee?

The Window Coffee

25 Wensum Street, Norwich NR3 1LA

www.thewindowcoffee.com
@TheWindowCoffee

Open

Tuesday – Saturday

Coffee from one of our favourite roasters in the UK – Has Bean, served up by one of the UK's top women baristas with fantastic freshly-baked pastries. Small but intimate, a wonderful coffee shop. How I envy the regulars.

More coffee?

Cleverdicks Coffee

14 All Saints Green, Norwich NR1 3NA

www.cleverdickscoffeeshop.co.uk
@cleverdickcoffe

Open

Monday – Saturday

You won't just get a Good Hair Day when you go to this coffee shop in Norwich. Unbeatable value, friendly service and a chat about Norwich City is as likely as a discussion of the latest celebrity look.

Tea?

The Tea House

5 Wrights Court, Norwich NR3 1HQ

Facebook: The Tea House Norwich
@teahousenorwich

Open

Monday – Saturday

Owner Chris not only has a passion for tea, he bakes his own cakes AND he's picked a great spot for a tea room, right by an antique clothes shop just off the cobbled Elm Hill. This is my top tip for tea in Norwich.

More tea?

Biddy's Tea Room

15 Lower Goat Lane, Norwich NR2 1EL

www.biddystearoom.com

Open

Daily

This a classic vintage tea room with fantastic cakes made by the 'gals' who work here. For a real retro experience, though, have your tea downstairs in the lounge area just behind the vintage retail section.

NOTTINGHAM CATHEDRAL OF
ST BARNABAS (CATHOLIC)

The founder of the Blue Nuns, Mary Potter, is entombed in the Lady Chapel at the east end of the church.

Stand in the middle of the nave and look east to the golden cross hanging in front of the beautiful rose window.

30 local martyrs are named on the wall of the Lady Chapel.

The initial of each of the apostles is set in the centre of the round murals lining the walls above the nave.

No admission charge and quite hard to find the little hole in the north wall where you can make a donation to the Cathedral restoration fund. The leaflet with a brief guided tour costs 25p!

Coffee?

Divine Coffee

Galleries of Justice Museum, High Pavement, Nottingham NG1 1HN

www.divinecoffee.co.uk
@divine_coffee

Open

Daily

Best coffee in Nottingham, we think. They moved recently into new premises within the Galleries of Justice Museum in Nottingham's historic Lace Market. We haven't visited the new venue, but the coffee and cake won't change, and the history of criminal England could be fun to see after your cuppa...

Tea?

White Rabbit Tea House

12 Hounds Gate, Nottingham NG1 7AB

www.whiterabbitteahouse.com
@wrteahouse

Open

Daily

Afternoon tea served on tiered cake trays and bone china in this little oasis of individuality tucked away behind Nottingham's main shopping streets. And a nice story of owner Frances, who packed in corporate life to achieve her dream of running her own tea room.

OBAN CATHEDRAL – ST COLUMBA'S (CATHOLIC)

The only cathedral in the country where you can take photos from the beach across the road; it was built to look out over Iona, which is the sacred isle of the Cathedral's patron saint.

Nice local connections, with the portrait of St Columba being chased over Loch Ness by Druids (over the entrance); and the carvings round the altar showing Saints meeting local Pictish people.

Much of the money to build the Cathedral came from exiled Highlanders living in the USA and Canada.

The Marquess of Bute commissioned the first cathedral on this spot in the 1880s: it was a corrugated iron building which stood for 50 years.

No recommended amount for donation.

OBAN CATHEDRAL – ST JOHN'S (EPISCOPAL)

The painting above the altar appears to show the Ascension happening in the Highlands of Scotland; the painted west windows show Jacob's Pillow being transported through Ireland to Western Scotland.

The eagle sculpture on the wall above the choir is impressive, all wings spread and claws poised.

The choir stalls are set out so that they look like a Celtic cemetery from afar.

A lifebelt from HMS Jason hangs in the nave; the ship was torpedoed in 1917 near the island of Coll, west of Oban.

No specific amount recommended for donations.

Coffee?

Dolce Vita

62 George Street, Oban PA34 5SD

www.dolcevitaoban.co.uk

Open

Daily

Best coffee we had in Oban and great views over the harbour from this coffee shop run by a true Italian-Scottish family, but make sure you ask them why there's a life-sized Native American Indian standing outside their angling shop round the corner...

Tea?

Julie's Coffee House

Stafford Street, Oban PA34 5NH

Open

Tuesday – Saturday (also Mondays in July/August/September)

Closed January to mid-February

The ladies who run this place tucked away behind the Oban Distillery have 200 different cake recipes from which they bake their daily cake. Fantastic quality cakes, and you can't go wrong with Suki Tea, loose-leaf and always good whatever the mood or the weather.

OXFORD CATHEDRAL – CHRIST CHURCH COLLEGE CHAPEL

Windows by the master of the pre-Raphaelites, Edward Burne-Jones, including the life of Oxford's patron saint Frideswide, but spot the flushing toilet in one of the window panels.

One of only two surviving Watching Lofts in the country (see St Albans for the other); used for keeping an eye on visiting pilgrims.

You can't miss the effigy of the 6'6" tall 14th century knight; must have been a giant in his day.

There's a rare surviving stained glass window depicting Thomas a Beckett, though his face was removed to save the window; and replaced in 1980 with a plain pink window.

Look for the 17th century graffiti around the tombs; seemed to be common practice around 1626-27.

There's a memorial stone to WH Auden in the remembrance chapel.

£8.50 charge to enter this cathedral and no guided tours, though some of the staff are very knowledgeable.

Coffee?

Zappi's Bike Café

28-32 St Michael's Street, Oxford OX1 2EB

www.zappisbikecafe.com
@zappiscafe

Open

Daily

You don't have to be a lycra-clad cyclist to enjoy this coffee shop upstairs above a bike shop, but if you do enjoy the Tour de France, you'll feel at home here. Don't worry, though, lots of locals and tourists find their way here for the great coffee and warm welcome.

More coffee?

The Missing Bean

14 Turl Street, Oxford OX1 3DQ

www.themissingbean.co.uk

Open

Daily

This coffee shop right opposite one of the Oxford colleges is inspired by the top quality coffee shops of Australia and New Zealand, but they've gone local for their coffee beans, being supplied by an Oxford-based roaster who uses a rather unique 'wood roast' method.

Tea?

The Rose Tea Room

51 High Street, Oxford OX1 4AS

www.the-rose.biz

Open

Daily

One of the only places in Oxford you'll find top quality loose-leaf tea. Recently taken on by an Albanian pair, who want to maintain the very English feel of this tea room – excellent cakes and scones baked in-house, too!

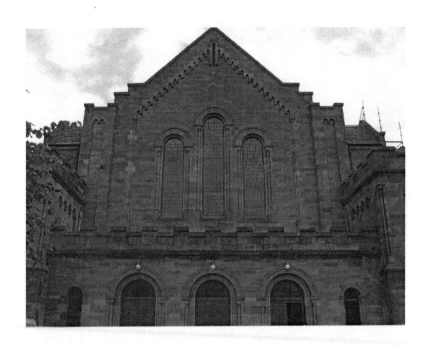

PAISLEY CATHEDRAL OF ST MIRIN (CATHOLIC)

No-one knows where St Mirin was buried. All that remains of him today is this cathedral in his name, a statue out the front, and of course the local football team: St Mirren…

This is one of the most simple, plain cathedrals you'll find in the UK, but also one of the more active, with 2,000 people attending mass each week.

No recommended amount but for £10 you can sponsor a roof slate in the ongoing re-roofing work…

Coffee?

Malatso Deli & Café

50 High Street, Paisley PA1 2DJ

Facebook: Deli Malatso

Open

Daily

This place gets our vote as best coffee shop in Paisley, not just for its good coffee and home-made cakes, but for the overall atmosphere, with the feel of a real local community hub, welcoming local musicians, knitters and a lot of other regulars.

Tea?

Sma' Shot Cottages Tea Room

Shuttle Street, Paisley PA1 1YD

http://www.smashot.co.uk/

Open

Wednesday and Saturday only (April to September only)

Best place in Paisley to get a feel for the town's weaving past. What a shame these lovingly restored weavers' cottages are so dependent on volunteer help to keep them open (and make the tea and cakes for visitors) – they're only open two days a week in summer, so plan your visit well!

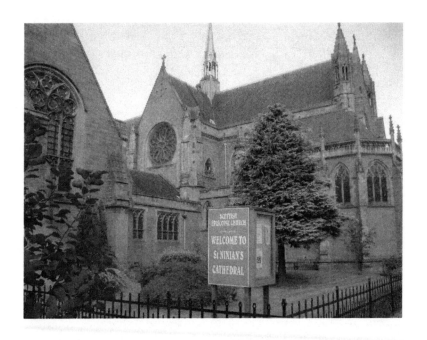

PERTH CATHEDRAL – ST NINIAN'S (EPISCOPAL)

Interesting links to Gothenburg, through the Carnegie family, which had yo-yo'ed back and forth to Sweden as generations got involved with politics (Bonnie Prince Charlie) and business; it's a Carnegie whose estate paid for the west window.

It was designed by the same architect as did the designs for Adelaide Cathedral in Australia.

Parts of the west window were blown out in a freak storm in January 2001 – now replaced, of course!

In 1850, this was the first cathedral to be built in Scotland since the Reformation.

There's an excellent but simple bullet-point outline of Scottish history along the wall as you enter this cathedral.

Any donation gratefully accepted.

Coffee?

Reid's Café

32-34 High Street, Perth PH1 5TQ

www.reidscafe.com

Open

Daily

Great coffee, roasted just a hundred yards up the road in central Perth. And if you're really lucky with the weather, you can sit outside on the terrace, continental style and watch the people of Perth going about their business.

Tea?

Deli – Cious

46 South Methven Street, Perth PH1 5NX

Facebook: Delicious

Open

Monday – Saturday

This place is great value, with top quality loose-leaf tea blended locally. Must be the most colourful café in town, too, and a really friendly welcome from the couple running the place.

PETERBOROUGH CATHEDRAL OF ST PETER, ST PAUL & ST ANDREW

Katharine of Aragon is buried here – you'll often see a pomegranate left on her tomb around the anniversary of her death.

Mary Queen of Scots was buried here before she was moved to Westminster Abbey.

'Old Scarlet' was the gravedigger who buried both queens: a wall painting of him survives above the west entrance.

Look up at the 13th century painted ceiling, with depictions of the 7 'liberal arts'.

Don't miss the complex of buildings that once made up the Benedictine monastery built around the Cathedral. Mostly remains but there was a refectory, dorm, table hall, cloisters…

Watch the old clock with 15th century parts. Never had a clock face, but used to chime the quarter hours and still ticks today.

Cromwell soldiers did more damage here than in any other cathedral (bar Lichfield) – see the Orme Memorial for evidence of the mess they left the building in...

Starbucks, just outside the cathedral quarter, stands on the site where ancient relics from Canterbury were on display in the 1200s and money was raised at a farthing per person to continue the building of the Cathedral.

John Betjeman supposedly wrote a poem about the St Spire Chapel – but he lost the cigarette packet on which he scribbled it!

No admission charge, but strong encouragement to leave a donation and £7 for the excellent daily tour.

Coffee?

The Butter Cross

Central Park, Park Crescent, Peterborough PE1 4DX

Open

Daily

Feel part of the community as soon as you walk into this café in the middle of Peterborough's Central Park. If you don't get a handshake from the owner's father, you'll almost certainly be made welcome by some of the other loyal customers who come here for a cuppa every day.

Tea?

Margaret's Tea Room

Wentworth Street, Peterborough PE1 1DH

www.margaretstearoom.com

Open

Monday – Saturday

The guys who run this tea room in central Peterborough blend their own tea and will recommend which tea to choose, depending on the mood you're in or the food you're eating. And if you want to feel a little bit special, try their Edward VIII blend, based on what was supposed to the favourite tea of the man himself!

PLYMOUTH CATHEDRAL – ST MARY & ST BONIFACE – CATHOLIC

The cobbled streets all around this part of Plymouth show how closely-knit the housing was near to the Cathedral, but you'll barely see a home built before the 1950s – most of them destroyed in the 59 bombing raids on the city during World War 2.

Highlight inside this cathedral is probably the west window, dedicated to Plymouth's patron saint, Boniface, it depicts his travels to Germany.

The 1st Bishop of Plymouth was actually from Richmond, North Yorkshire, but he never saw this cathedral built; there's far more about the 2nd Bishop, who was around for most of the second half of the 19th century – he saw the Cathedral built and opened by 1858.

The Bishop's Throne is a very plain, simple and modern-designed chair; no ostentatious soft luxury, here.

No recommended amount for donation, but you can buy a guide to the Cathedral for £3.

Coffee?

coffee bean plymouth

12 Cornwall Street, Plymouth PL1 1LP

Facebook: coffee bean plymouth
@coffeebeaninfo

Open

Daily

If you want a cosy coffee experience in an independent coffee shop with a decent cuppa (tea, coffee or hot chocolate), this is the place to go in Plymouth. Very handy for the shops, too!

Tea?

Tudor Rose Tea Rooms

36 New Street, Plymouth PL1 2NA

www.tudorrosetearoom.co.uk

Open

Daily

If buildings could talk, you'd get a few stories from this one: a wealthy linen merchant lived here in the 1640s; but by the 1850s, 68 people lived here in poverty. It's been a tea room now for 20 years and it's a fantastic spot for a real Devonshire Cream Tea.

PORTSMOUTH CATHEDRAL (ST THOMAS)

The original Cathedral here was built right on the harbour, so where the nave is today may well have been under water in the 12th century!

A copy of the marriage certificate of Charles II and Catherine of Braganca is on display in the north aisle – she was the Portuguese princess credited with making tea fashionable in English society (they married in the Garrison Church round the corner).

There's a cannon ball lying up near the altar, probably fired by parliamentarian troops based in nearby Gosport during the Civil War (Portsmouth remained staunchly Royalist).

A section of a flag from Nelson's HMS Victory is on display in the Naval Chapel – and its frame is of oak from the ship itself.

A memorial stone to the crew of the Mary Rose lies on the floor of the Naval Chapel, installed after the ship's hull was brought to the surface in the 1980s.

Lovers of Dickens should look out for the stained glass window high in the north wall of St Thomas's Chapel; the father of the Mr Gaselee portrayed in the window became Stareleigh in *Pickwick Papers*.

The peace globe, where you can light a candle for peace, is based on an idea in Stockholm Cathedral.

Entrance is free but a recommended donation of at least £2.

PORTSMOUTH CATHOLIC CATHEDRAL (ST JOHN'S)

Not surprising they needed a Catholic Cathedral in Portsmouth, this being an old garrison town and the proportion of Catholics in the armed forces being much higher than average (about 30% back in the 19th century, when this cathedral was built).

The Lady Chapel has rather splendid paintings of saints 'relevant' to Portsmouth; and the ceiling above the nave is about as clear as any nave ceiling can be in depicting the shape of a boat hull.

The land was bought from the War Department when Portsmouth's defences were improved in the 1870s.

It's hard to defend against aerial bombing, though, and this cathedral suffered damage in 1941 air raids, when the Bishop's Palace next door was demolished.

The Arundel-based Duke of Norfolk was the main benefactor listed as paying for the construction of the Cathedral, but who were the Baron Roeslager and Countess Tasker?

No recommendations for donations.

Coffee?

Manna Tea Room

39 High Street, Old Portsmouth PO1 2LU

http://mannatearoom.co.uk/home.html

Open

Daily

You won't find a better spot for views of Portsmouth Cathedral; and you'll have to travel a long way to find a nicer piece of cake (all baked in-house, moist and spongy). They call themselves a tea room but they get our vote for best coffee round here.

Tea?

T on the Quay

35 Broad Street, Old Portsmouth PO1 2JD

http://www.broadstreet35.co.uk/gallery.html

Open

Daily (June to September only)

A good pot of Yorkshire Tea in a 17th century building right by the old harbour where so many of the great and good (and bad) have embarked for foreign lands over the centuries. Mind you, Catherine de Braganca landed near here, too, so there are historical tea connections...

Cuppa near the other cathedral?

The Park Café

The Lodge Arts Centre, Victoria Park, Anglesea Road, Portsmouth PO1 3HJ

www.artandsoultraders.com

Open

Daily

A very handy spot for a cuppa if you're visiting the RC Cathedral or fancy a stroll in the park while waiting for your train (at Portsmouth & Southsea!). But this is worth a visit anyway, just to see who the Artful Lodgers are...

RIPON CATHEDRAL

The 672AD crypt is all that remains of the original Saxon church on this site; most of the Cathedral was built in the 12th century – a transition period between round Norman arches and pointed Gothic, so a real mixture of styles throughout.

> Lewis Carroll's Dad was a canon here. Some of the wood carvings in the choir stalls are said to have inspired Alice in Wonderland characters; and spot the Cheshire Cat carved later to mark Lewis Carroll's presence…

George Washington's family arms are in a stained glass window on the north wall: were these a blueprint for the Stars & Stripes?

> They say the monkey carved on the end of the Mayor's seat in the choir (opposite the Bishop's throne) had something to do with the first mayor's personality…

The stone tombs of knights in armour from 1398 are pretty impressive (reminding us of scenes from Monty Python…).

Women used to be made to squeeze through a hole in the crypt before weddings to 'prove their chastity'!

No admission charge and not even a suggested amount – but this cathedral is well worth a donation!

Coffee?

Oliver's Pantry

86 North Street, Ripon HG4 1DP

http://www.oliverspantry.com/
@oliverspantry

Open

Daily

The best place for coffee in Ripon, not just because it's a quality coffee, but also because of the wonderful atmosphere and the way the owners have renovated the building, while preserving part of its history as a ginger beer bottling factory! Cakes are pretty nice, too.

Tea?

Tiggy's Tea Room

6-7 High Skellgate, Ripon HG4 1BA

Open

Monday – Saturday

The family takes centre stage in this tea room. Owner Tiggy Ferris's father was a mayor in nearby Harrogate a few decades ago and his photos are on the wall; Tiggy's 87 year old Mum still makes the jams for the cream tea; and Tiggy herself has been catering for large numbers ever since she was a little girl on a local farm!

ROCHESTER CATHEDRAL

No surprise to find a memorial plaque to Charles Dickens, given how many characters and buildings he based on Rochester; some of the names on even older memorial stones make you wonder if he used the Cathedral as a source of ideas for his characters' names.

Highlight of Rochester Cathedral has to be the 14th century wall painting, in vivid reds and golds, which survived Henry VIII's destruction by being hidden behind a heavy oak chair near the quire – it was discovered in 1825.

Beautiful Norman arches line the nave, though if you look closely at the west end of the church you'll see the copper lines in the floor, marking the chancel of the original 7th century Saxon cathedral.

The oldest window in the Cathedral is tucked away in the north east corner – it's tiny, with yellow glass and so clearly older than any of the other stained glass in the Cathedral.

The Pilgrims' Steps are covered now in a protective layer of wood but you can still see the curve of the stone where thousands of pilgrims came to see the shrine of the martyred baker, William of Perth.

The 14th century doorway to the south east side of the quire was the old night entrance for the monks to enter the Cathedral for prayers – I wonder how many of the elaborate carvings they noticed in the dead of night...

The Cathedral marked its 1,400th anniversary in 2004 by commissioning Russian artist Fyodorov to paint the mural by the north door directly onto wet plaster.

No recommended amount for donation.

Coffee?

Deaf Cat Café

83 High Street, Rochester ME1 1LX

www.thedeafcat.com

Open

Daily

This place has all the ingredients for an excellent independent coffee shop: great coffee beans; lovely espresso machine; quality local milk; and cakes baked locally too. There's a quirky Dickens connection and even the owner has a fascinating family history involving boxing and Australia...

Tea?

Peggottys

81a High Street, Rochester, Kent ME1 1LX – upstairs above the hardware store

Open

Daily

Surround yourself with portraits of Dickens characters in this tea room with great views of Rochester Cathedral. The building has been a pub, a jeweller's, a dowser's, a milliner's and now a hardware store downstairs. They do a lovely cream tea here and the cakes are all baked in-house.

SALFORD CATHEDRAL (CATHOLIC)

There are sketches of Pope John Paul II dating from his visit to Manchester in 1982; they are surrounded by the text of the Bishop of Salford's welcome to the Pope.

> The foundation stone for the Cathedral was laid in 1844, which just happens to be the year that Marx & Engels were in town to research *The Condition of the Working Class in England* – I wonder if they attended the ceremony...

The Cathedral is built on a north-south axis, which means the sun can shine for hours through the 'west' window, making it hard to see the modern, abstract stained glass – rare to see such pale colours in a cathedral window.

> The memorial chapel to those who died in World War One is extraordinary for the sheer number of names listed on 7 panels; some died as late as 1920, presumably from war wounds, or maybe from action in the Russian Civil War?

No recommended amount for donation.

Coffee?

Tower Coffee Shop

The Lowry, Pier 8, Salford Quays, M50 3AZ

http://www.thelowry.com/plan-your-visit/eat-and-drink/tower-coffee-shop/

Open

Daily

I wonder what LS Lowry would make of the Salford Quays development. He'd probably be hanging out in this coffee shop people-watching, though the landscape and style has changed a little since he was alive…

Tea?

Lark Hill Tea Shop

Salford Museum & Art Gallery, Salford M5 4WU

http://www.salford.gov.uk/cafe.htm
@SalfordMuseum

Open

Daily

Step back in time to Salford's past when you go for a cuppa in the museum's tea room. This is a great little find in my favourite building in old Salford: the museum was a mansion house for a wealthy family once upon a time!

SALISBURY CATHEDRAL

The original Salisbury Cathedral was two miles north of the modern-day town, at Old Sarum. If you've never experienced ley-lines, go there and just feel its significance going back thousands of years.

The 'modern' cathedral dates from 1258, some 43 years after the signing of Salisbury Cathedral's greatest treasure: the Magna Carta (actually signed on the Thames near Windsor, but displayed here because of a local earl who played a key role in getting King John to sign it).

The clock dates from the 14th century (they claim it's the oldest in Europe), but it has no face to tell the time; it rings a bell every hour, so folk knew when to come to services...

Get one of the guides to show you the stone in the cathedral floor which is lifted to check the water levels below ground (too low and the Cathedral may sink into its gravel base; too high and it floods!).

The font was installed in 2008 to mark the Cathedral's 750th anniversary; make sure you give it time and see the reflection of the nave arches in the water.

The cloisters were never part of a monastery, but were used as a Prisoner of War camp for Dutch captives during the Anglo-Dutch wars of the 17th and 18th centuries.

Former Prime Minister Edward Heath lived across the close and has a memorial stone above his ashes in the floor of the Cathedral.

There's a Donations Desk as you enter and the recommended donation is £6.50. No obligation to donate but this place is so special you may be moved to leave more.

Coffee?

Bird & Carter

3 Fish Row, Salisbury SP1 1EX

www.birdandcarter.co.uk

Open

Daily

This 15th century building has wonderful old beams gnawed away by mediaeval woodworm. Great place to sit and munch on the home-baked cakes and sip what we think is the best coffee in Salisbury.

Tea?

The Yard

16 Dews Road, Salisbury SP2 7SN

www.theyardsalisbury.com

Open

Tuesday – Saturday

Fancy a pot of tea and a piece of home-baked cake away from all the tourists in Salisbury? Pop along to The Yard, where this mother and daughter team have set up a lovely café and art gallery in a building that was originally a funeral director's!

SHEFFIELD CATHEDRAL OF ST PETER & ST PAUL

The tower, central pillars and part of the roof date from the 1430s, but most of the church is Victorian.

Until 1931, the protestant church always had a Catholic chapel, and in 2011-12 during reconstruction of the Catholic Cathedral in town, it also welcomed Catholic worship.

One of the flags in the Regimental Chapel saw action in the American War of Independence (on the British side, of course!).

Check out the tomb of the 6th Earl of Shrewsbury: he was custodian of Mary Queen of Scots in Sheffield for 14 years – was he the first person to sleep on a backpacker's bed-roll?

Look out for the small window deep in the Crypt. Made from perspex cylinders glued together. Beautiful colours.

HMS Sheffield's original silk flag flies in the Regimental

Chapel, and the ship's bell hangs by the font – recognition of what was used for baptisms at sea...

The 4th Earl of Shrewsbury lies with both his wives. The tomb was commissioned by his 2nd wife, who recognised the importance of both ladies in his life.

In the 18th century, Sheffield's fire engine used to be housed where the St Katharine Chapel is now.

No admission charge and no suggested amount.

SHEFFIELD CATHEDRAL OF ST MARIE (CATHOLIC)

This 19th century cathedral was completely renovated in 2012 – rededication in November 2012. During the restoration work, some 15th century carvings were found, which had been donated to the church when it was built in the 1840s.

The founder of the church, Father Pratt, died aged 38 before the building was complete, but a stone figure of Fr Pratt lies by the altar still today, clutching the cathedral he never saw.

During the War, the stained glass windows were removed and buried down a nearby mine shaft for safe-keeping; the mine flooded during the war and it took two years to retrieve the mud-covered glass and replace it in the windows.

Don't miss the painted tiles in both the north and south walls in memory of members of the congregation who died between 1850 and 1882.

Coffee?

Tamper Coffee

9 Westfield Terrace, Sheffield S1 4GH

www.tampercoffee.co.uk

Facebook: Tamper Coffee
Twitter: @tampercoffee

Open

Daily

Grab a bit of Kiwi coffee culture in this cosy little coffee shop in Sheffield which would certainly come in our 50 best coffee shops in the UK. Some say the milk's as important as the coffee in making a good cappuccino, and they get theirs delivered daily from a farm a few miles away.

More coffee?

Bragazzi's Deli and Café

224-226 Abbeydale Road, Sheffield S7 1FL

www.bragazzis.co.uk

Open

Daily

There's a real Italian feel to this place, with the pasta, cheese and oils for sale in the deli next door. Their coffee is roasted locally in Sheffield, though. So they blend the global and the local beautifully.

Tea?

Honey Pie Tea Room

115-117 Chesterfield Road, Sheffield S8 0RN

Facebook: Honey Pie Tearoom
Twitter: @honeypietearoom

Open

Tuesday – Saturday

Owner Jo's aim is to 'bring people together through the power of tea and cake'. It helps when you bake all the cakes yourself and they're deliciously moist; and when your loose-leaf teas are supplied by a local Sheffield-based blender. Lovely spot for afternoon tea, about a mile out of the city centre.

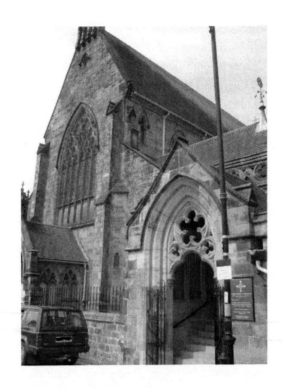

SHREWSBURY CATHEDRAL – OUR LADY & ST PETER OF ALCANTARA

Roman Catholic Cathedral built in 1840s, just after it became legal again for Catholics to worship in England.

Look out for the London bus – 1921 model – in one of the stained glass windows; apparently there's an Olympic swimmer too somewhere but we couldn't find it!

Margaret Rope designed most of the stained glass before she became a Carmelite nun.

The original plans for the Cathedral had a tall spire, but this could never be built because of the building's weak foundations.

There is a donation box, but no recommended amount.

Coffee?

Shrewsbury Coffee House

5 Castle Gates, Shrewsbury SY1 2AE

www.shrewsburycoffeehouse.co.uk
@coffeehouseltd

Open

Daily

The owner of this coffee shop near Shrewsbury's mediaeval walls shows how a diverse life story can culminate in a top venue for a cuppa. Jess was brought up in Texas, but worked in the UK in interior design, jam-making and catering before putting her creative mind to coffee. She chose top-quality coffee from Stafford and cakes made in her Mum's bakery – this is one of our favourite independent coffee shops.

Afternoon tea?

Camellia's Tea Rooms

Prince Rupert Hotel

St Alkmund's Square, Shrewsbury SY1 1UQ

www.prince-rupert-hotel.co.uk/en/restaurants/camellias-tea-rooms/index/php

Open

Tuesday – Saturday

If it's the tradition of English Afternoon Tea that brought you to this tea room in Shrewsbury, you must pop your head round the door of the 12th century hotel next door. It's owned by the same couple as run the tea room, so have a look round the reception area and imagine some of the mediaeval celebrities who may have been there before you.

SOUTHWARK CATHEDRAL

Southwark sees itself as the 'People's Cathedral' and you're as likely to find a memorial to a coal merchant, a grocer, a dyer or a hop factor as you are a local dignitary.

Don't miss the memorial in the cathedral gardens to Chief Mahomet, who died of smallpox, having come to England from America in 1735 to claim back stolen lands; Bruce Two Dogs Bozsum had to be buried in Southwark because foreigners could not be buried in the City of London.

The Harvard Chapel commemorates the founder of Harvard University – he was baptised here in 1607.

Shakespeare's monument was paid for by British and American 'admirers' in 1911; can you spot the Mick Jagger look-alike in the actors' window above? (Thanks to the Day Chaplain for pointing him out...).

Look out for the Cathedral cat wandering the place: called Magnificat.

Look for the stained glass window paid for by 670 working class parishioners in Victorian days in thanks to the local surgeon.

Also worth looking for: the chapel in memory of HIV/AIDS sufferers; and the memorial to the victims of the Marchioness boat disaster in 1989; Chaucer's window.

Recommended donation of at least £4.

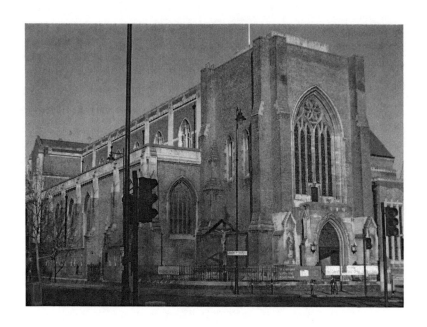

ST GEORGE'S CATHEDRAL, SOUTHWARK
(ROMAN CATHOLIC)

The congregation today reflects the diverse mix of communities living in this part of London; and appropriately there is a shrine to the patron saint of migrants, tucked away in the north wall.

Bombing raids in 1941 virtually destroyed the building, only small sections remaining when the new church was opened in 1958.

Pope John Paul II was here in 1982 and a stained glass window in the north east corner of the building commemorates his visit.

The Dalai Lama visited the Cathedral in 1994, after a formal stop by the Tibetan Peace Garden in the Imperial War Museum across the road.

The Venerable Mary Potter spent the first 18 years of her life living in this parish – her connection to the Cathedral is marked by a photo near the entrance.

No recommended amount for donations but they 'will make a very real difference'.

Coffee?

Monmouth Coffee

2 Park Street, London SE1 9AB

www.monmouthcoffee.co.uk

Open

Monday – Saturday

There's a good reason why the queue outside Monmouth lasts from opening time through to closure at 6pm:- the coffee here is just very good and worth waiting for. Roasted just down the road in Bermondsey, it couldn't be fresher either.

Tea?

teapod @ the Fashion & Textile Museum

83 Bermondsey Street, London SE1 3XF

http://teapodtea.co.uk
@teapodlondon

Open

Daily

You can't get a more stylish venue than the Fashion & Textile Museum for a good pot of quality loose-leaf tea. And the media-savvy owner of this tea room gets involved each year with the BBC's Comic Relief.

SOUTHWELL MINSTER

The original cathedral was built over 900 years ago in 1108 (fantastic Norman arches), but traces of the original Saxon church floor can be seen in the South Transept, with some Roman mosaic tiles.

The stained glass in the East window is thought to come from a church in Paris (Temple district) which was ransacked after the Revolution; it was bought by a local MP from a Paris junk shop in the 1820s!

The 16th century brass eagle lectern in the choir was retrieved from a pond where it had been thrown by fleeing monks during Henry VIII's reign...

A stained glass window in the North Transept marks the 200th anniversary of the Bramley Apple, first grown down the road in Southwell.

Look out for the man with toothache carved into the wall of the passageway to the Chapter House.

Don't miss the 1788 list of donations to the poor of Southwell

(North Wall), or the Bread Pews (South Transept) where the poor would sit and wait for bread to be given.

There's a painted Roman wall plaster on the South Wall; and an old Saxon stone carving in the North Transept.

Check out the green men in the Chapter House and imagine mediaeval days when all the carvings would have been coloured...green!

Don't miss the peppercorn towers, but also note the Victorian stained glass window which has the peppercorns missing (they were rebuilt 30 years after the window was made).

No admission charge but a recommended donation of £5, and a good audio tour for £5.

Coffee?

Alfresco Caffe

10 Queen Street, Southwell NG25 0AA

www.alfrescocaffe.com

Open

Monday – Saturday

A little bit of Italy comes to Southwell, not only with the coffee, but in the cakes, the pasta, the Italian conversation classes and the whole décor of this coffee shop right in the centre of town. Maurizio is your man.

Tea?

The Old Theatre Deli

4 Market Place, Southwell NG25 0HE

www.theoldtheatredeli.com

Open

Daily

There's excellent loose-leaf tea and freshly-baked cakes to be had in this beautiful deli, housed downstairs from an old Georgian theatre in the heart of Southwell. Take a peek upstairs at the old stage and theatre adverts even if you have tea outside on the market place.

ST ALBANS CATHEDRAL
(ALSO CALLED ST ALBANS ABBEY)

There's been a church on this site for 1,700 years.

The 15th century wooden watching chamber was designed to keep an eye on pilgrims visiting St Alban's shrine and make sure they behaved themselves; don't miss the bear-baiters and wrestlers carved in the side walls.

The only English Pope, Adrian IV, was a local lad, born in the early 12th century – a carving of him appears near the altar, and he has a named stall in the choir.

Lots of deep red wall paintings from as early as the 12th century; as usual de-faced in Henry VIII's time.

Look out for the flags of the US, France, Italy, Belgium and the image of Joan of Arc in the west window, commemorating the world war dead.

The sculptures of martyrs in the nave screen include Oscar Romero from El Salvador and a protestant baker from Yorkshire,

George Tankerfield; an earlier sculpture of Martin Luther King didn't make the final choice but is he still to be found elsewhere in the Cathedral?

Local school kids made the tapestry-frieze depicting the history of the Abbey from its inception to the 14th century.

Spot the snails carved into the walls of the Chantry Chapel, sliding among the vines...

Recommended donation of £4; the excellent guided tours are free.

Coffee?

bakehouse stalbans

17 Heritage Close, St Albans AL3 4EB

www.localbakehouse.co.uk
@BakehouseStA

Open

Daily

With cakes made in the in-house bakery and coffee from Monmouth in London, this place oozes quality; and if you want views of St Albans Abbey (cathedral) over your cuppa, you can't miss this coffee shop in the centre of St Albans.

Commuter coffee?

Soko Coffee

By the Platform 4 exit to St Albans City Station

www.sokocoffee.co.uk

@SokoCoffee

Open

Monday – Friday (till 10am)

Don't fancy commuting to London from St Albans? Well, if you knew how good the coffee was next to Platform 4, you might even look for a job that takes you through St Albans train station in the morning. HasBean coffee and a cheerful smile Monday to Friday!

Tea?

Tea for Two

Fleetville Vintage Emporium, 221 Hatfield Road, St Albans AL1 4TB

www.thefleetvillevintageemporium.co.uk

Open

Daily

Best place for a pot of tea round St Albans surely has to be at this tea room in the Fleetville Vintage Emporium. Lovely loose-leaf tea, home-baked cakes and if you like the table and chairs you're sitting at, they're all vintage or retro and they'll have a price tag on them – take-aways with a difference!

ST ASAPH CATHEDRAL

There's a 1588 Welsh translation of the Bible in the Cathedral's Translators Chapel.

They reckon the little Madonna in a niche in the cathedral wall was washed up from the Spanish Armada, also in 1588.

There's an intimate warmth to the cathedral choir, where the Canons' stalls were made in 1482 – spot the face of the carver (they think) above the stall for David op Howel.

During Cromwell's time, the church was used for housing horses and oxen; the font was a watering trough down by the river.

The Deacon's chair and that of the Resident Canon are almost as big as the Bishop's throne...

No recommended amount for donation, but you leave coins in a 1738 iron chest – just a shame it's padded, so you can't hear the tinkle of coins dropping in.

Coffee?

Jacobs Ladder Coffee Shop

Mount Road, St Asaph LL17 0DB

Facebook: Jacobs Ladder

Open

Monday – Saturday

With the cathedral just across the road, this lovely coffee shop in St Asaph is perfectly-placed for a great cuppa and cake on our UK cathedral coffee tour. Such a good vibe to this place, too, made even better by wonderful home-baked cakes.

Tea?

We have nowhere else to recommend for tea in St Asaph, so suggest you just go back to Jacobs Ladder in the afternoon...

ST DAVIDS CATHEDRAL

Pope Calixtus II is supposed to have said that two visits to St Davids Cathedral are worth one visit to Rome, so this was an important place even in 1123.

Henry VIII didn't ransack the place because he chose it for the resting place of his granddad – the tomb is still in the Cathedral today.

One story has it that the Cathedral was built here because of the fast-running stream nearby; another says that they built it tucked away in the valley to hide it from any sea-based attackers. Trouble is, the tower was visible from a point 1 ½ miles out to sea, so that idea didn't work...

The Sapphire Stone looks fairly unremarkable, set in a plain wooden table, but they say this was the very stone carried by St David as his portable altar and brought back to Wales from the Middle East...

The walls of St Davids Cathedral lean out, meaning the ceiling is wider than the floor – this is due to the steepness of the original stone roof.

We loved the coins in the Treasury, some dating from Edward III's days (1327-77), some more recent, from the Queen's Maundy Money distribution in 1982.

We were also intrigued by the book of Welsh law in the Treasury, where we learnt that "Dead fish in the ocean all belong to the King", but there was no hint as to what he might do with them…

Recommended donation £3.

Coffee?

Pebbles Yard Espresso Bar

Cross Square, St Davids SA62 6RD

www.pebblesyard.co.uk

Open

Daily (closed in January)

St Davids is lucky to have such a nice little coffee shop with good coffee and lovely home-baked cakes. Great space, too, shared with a local artist/photographer.

Tea?

The Sampler Tea Room

17 Nun Street, St Davids SA62 6NS

http://www.sampler-tearoom.co.uk/

Open

Monday – Wednesday (March – November only)

You're surrounded by samplers (embroidery pieces) in this lovely tea room close to the beautiful cathedral and Bishop's palace. Lots of local food, some so local it's grown in the garden behind the house and a great loose-leaf brew.

STEVENAGE COPTIC CATHEDRAL OF ST GEORGE

The first cathedral in the UK to be purpose-built for the Coptic Church.

The Cathedral was locked on the day of our visit but we managed to see through the windows:

Beautiful gold-coloured icons above the main altar.

The only cathedral which appeared to have a basketball court set up in its nave.

Coffee?

Deluxe Espresso Bar

7 Middle Row, Old Town Stevenage SG1 3AN

Facebook: Deluxe Espresso
@Deluxe_Espresso

Open

Tuesday – Sunday

Coffee smooth and well-presented; cakes baked in-house fresh every day. And lots of room for parents with kids to hang out, including a play area at the back. All this in a lovely 300 year-old building in Old Stevenage.

More Coffee or tea maybe?

Gladleys Deli-Café

Middle Row, Old Town Stevenage SG1 3AN

www.gladleys.co.uk

Open

Daily

This deli and café in Old Stevenage sits just off where the Great North Road used to run and 22 stagecoaches a day would pass through on their way to and from London. The horses used to be led past what is now the counter to the stables out the back: it's more peaceful now you can stop here for a cuppa and a piece of home-baked cake.

SWANSEA CATHEDRAL OF ST JOSEPH (CATHOLIC)

The Greenhill district of Swansea, on which this church was built in 1886, was described by the resident priest as a 'sordid spot' on a hillside with no roads, streets or lighting; the aim was to build a church that would lift people's thoughts heavenwards…

> The site on which the Cathedral stands was once a deep hole filled with water, so its foundations dig as deep down as the walls rise up.

Look out for the stained glass window from the original church, depicting a Father carrying a model of the schools which still stand next to the Cathedral.

> The relics of St Desiderius are apparently inserted into the altar; he was persecuted in AD305 in Italy and beheaded after wild beasts in the amphitheatre didn't touch him…

No amount recommended for donation, so why not buy one of the £2 history pamphlets, either on the Greenhill district and the building of the church, or on the symbolism of the windows and statues?

Coffee?

Kardomah Coffee House

11 Portland Street, Swansea SA1 3DH

http://www.kardomahcoffeeshop.co.uk/

Open

Daily

Home of the 'Kardomah Gang' when Dylan Thomas was around, this place is so fashionably retro that Dr Who flew in when they wanted the Tardis to land in 1950s Britain. And the same family has run the place for 42 years – now that's what I call continuity in coffee.

More coffee?

Cove Coffee

36 Castle Street, Swansea SA1 1HZ

Facebook: The Cove

Open

Monday – Saturday

This stylish, contemporary coffee shop takes Swansea's coffee scene into the 21st century, with a quality cuppa, relaxing atmosphere and local artists displaying their work on the walls.

Tea?

The Kitchen Table

626 Mumbles Road, Mumbles, Swansea SA3 4EA

http://www.thekitchentablecafe.co.uk
@Kitchtablecafe

Open

Daily

The tea and cakes are so good and the village of Mumbles so full of character, it's worth the hike around Swansea Bay to get to this place. And if you want inspiration for a total life change, chat to the owners of this café, who started out selling burgers in a London market...

TRURO CATHEDRAL

Not often you get a church within a church. But the St Mary Aisle, with its Cornish barrel ceiling, and its original 17th century organ, was part of the mediaeval church on this site. They just added the much bigger Cathedral to it 600 years later.

Edward VII laid the foundation stone when he was still Prince of Wales in 1880. Is that why the sculptor who carved the terracotta Way of the Cross (in the north aisle) made Pontius Pilate a dead ringer for Edward?

There's a wonderful painting showing the whole diocese of Truro, with a Celtic cross for each parish church, and the arrival of Celtic saints from Ireland on the horizon. Well they do say, apparently, that there are more saints in Cornwall than in heaven...

Don't miss the matchstick model of the Cathedral. Made in 1999, after 1,600 hours of work, it used over 42,000 matches!

Can you spot the single blue window in the East Window stained glass? It's a replacement for one window broken by a lad with an air rifle. They call it their only war damage.

The RNLI flag by the West entrance is hung on a pole made from the wreckage of the Solomon Browne, which sank off the Cornish coast in 1981, losing all hands.

Most impressive object? The tombs of wealthy 17th century merchant John Robartes and his wife Phillipe (or did they mean Phillipa?).

Entrance to this cathedral is free. But they encourage you to buy the £3 guidebook...

Coffee?

108 Coffee

108 Kenwyn Street, Truro TR1 3DJ

www.108coffee.co.uk
@108_coffee

Open

Monday – Saturday

I loved the way the young couple who run this coffee shop in the centre of Truro learnt their trade in the coffee shops close to Sydney's beaches in Australia. Truro's not on the beach but you can feel the Aussie influence in this stylish place with excellent coffee.

Tea?

Charlotte's Tea House

1 Boscawen Street, Truro TR1 2QU

Open

Monday – Saturday

It's not often you get the chance in England to drink loose-leaf tea that was grown just five miles away. So when you go for afternoon tea in this beautiful tea room overlooking Truro's main street, it's worth paying the few pence extra to enjoy the experience. Tregothnan's the tea…

WAKEFIELD CATHEDRAL

Wakefield Cathedral has the tallest spire in Yorkshire, at 75m (247ft).

The writer of the song the 'Lambeth Walk' – Noel Gay – was a chorister here as a teenager.

The Chantry Chapel – owned by the Cathedral, but 10 minutes walk away – is one of only three remaining chapels built on bridges in England; built in the 1340s.

During the time the Chantry Chapel was closed to acts of worship it became a cheesecake store and later a newsroom – nice windows for the editorial staff!

Wonderful stained glass windows in the Cathedral – look for the image of Joseph carrying a miner's lamp…

Beautiful carved owl in the choir – dated 1482.

Replica of the original Wakefield cross from 940AD.

No admission charge here but a poetic encouragement to donate: "Our spire is tall, our funds are low; Please don't be shy, just have a go; Throw us your change, whether pence or pounds; Aim at the bell, and make it sound" – and a nice chime when the coin hits the bell...

Coffee?

Mocca Moocho

10 Cross Square, Wakefield WF1 1PQ

Facebook: Mocca Moocho Wakefield

Open

Daily

For lovely views of the cathedral, good coffee and fabulous home-baked cakes, we strongly recommend this family-run independent coffee shop right in the heart of Wakefield.

Tea?

The Conservatory Tea Rooms

36 Little Westgate, Wakefield WF1 1JY

Open

Monday – Saturday

This tea room used to be a hairdressing salon many years ago and we hear that a couple of the ladies in their 90s who take tea here these days used to come here for their haircuts as young gals! It's been a tea room now for over 20 years, with beautiful stained glass windows, tea pots on the walls and prettily-laid tables. Get here by 3pm, though!

WELLS CATHEDRAL (ST ANDREW'S)

The astronomical clock with the jousting knights is Wells' star attraction. Made in 1392, it has extraordinary accuracy even today, marking the time of the lunar month as well as the hours and minutes. Lots more jousting at midday than at 1pm, obviously, so choose your time well.

> The 46 houses on the beautiful Vicars Close are directly connected to the Cathedral. They were built in the 1350s for each of the 46 canons, to make sure they had no excuse for being late for prayers!

The font dates from the 10th century Saxon Cathedral whose site overlapped with the current building, explaining why the font stands in the south transept rather than by the cathedral entrance.

> The stained glass at the east end of the Cathedral survived the destruction of the Reformation, mainly – they say – because the guy who was knocking out the panes from windows further to

the west, leant back too far to admire his work and came to a nasty end on the floor of the church.

The scissors-shaped arch in the nave is unique and fairly modern-looking, although it was made in 1338. Its purpose was to shore up the building, but some say the design was aimed at symbolising the cross of St Andrew.

Look out for the carved figures in the pillars of the south transept: one has toothache, like the carving in Southwell Minster; and one is picking a thorn from the sole of his feet.

Fantastic graffiti on two of the 14th century effigies, mostly dating from the 16th and 17th centuries, when signing your name on the tombs of revered people was thought to bring you closer to God.

Don't miss the Chapter House, with its intricate webbing in the ceiling. Surely the only upstairs Chapter House in the country?

Recommended donation of £6 – well worth it with the excellent free guided tour.

Coffee?

Strangers with Coffee

31 St Cuthbert Street, Wells BA5 2AW

Facebook: Strangers with Coffee

Open

Monday – Saturday

The guys who run this fantastic little coffee shop in Wells think they may serve the best coffee in the south west. They might just be right! This is a cosy place with lots of style, a very positive outlook on the world, and a great local customer base which includes a number of well-known explorers and adventurers!

Tea?

We didn't find anywhere we could recommend for tea in Wells. However, we hear good things about a place a few miles away in Cheddar (yes, the home of the cheese!). The Tea Guild has a member there: Derrick's Tea House (shame it was closed when we dropped by).

WESTMINSTER CATHEDRAL OF
THE MOST PRECIOUS BLOOD

This is the mother of all Catholic cathedrals in England and Wales.

Don't be put off by the dark ceiling as you enter: this cathedral was designed to be unfinished, leaving future generations to continue the work; if it's colour you want go straight to the St Gregory & St Augustine Chapel in the south aisle.

Elgar's Dream of Gerontius was first performed in this cathedral – look out for the plaques to commemorate this.

It's not clear why the English, Scottish and Irish saints (George, Andrew & Patrick) had chapels named after them, but St David just got a mosaic panel (however beautiful that mosaic may be…).

Don't miss the shrine of St John Southworth, who ministered in the 17th century, when it was illegal to do so as a Catholic, and who was hung, drawn and quartered at Tyburn Gallows (Marble Arch) in 1654 for his efforts.

Donations asked for but not required.

Coffee?

Flat Cap Coffee Company

Strutton Ground (Great Peter Street end)

London SW1P 2HR

@FlatCapVictoria

Open

Monday – Friday

Fantastic Square Mile coffee from a pop-up coffee shop in the heart of Westminster. But don't look for this place after 5pm or at the weekends; they pack it all up and store it away till the next morning, lock, stock and kitchen sink…

Tea?

St Ermin's Hotel

2 Caxton Street, London SW1H 0QW

@sterminshotel
http://www.sterminshotel.co.uk/

Open

Daily (Afternoon Tea from 1-5pm but a pot of tea anytime)

What more could you ask for in a tea venue? Excellent loose-leaf tea, quality food on a tiered platter for Afternoon Tea; lots of history with spy stories and wartime bravery; and a 21st century sustainable touch with 200,000 bees on the roof providing honey that goes into the cakes and scones for your tea.

WINCHESTER CATHEDRAL

Alfred the Great's body was originally buried here, but it was moved. Look up at the mortuary chests perched above the nave. They contain the remains of other Saxon kings, maybe even including King Cnut (or Canute), but we don't know for sure since Henry VIII's guys tossed the bones all over the place...

Jane Austen seems to be the biggest celebrity these days, even though she only spent a short time here before she died. Big plaque for her, big window, and a stone in the floor which remembers the 'extraordinary endowments of her mind', but does not refer to her writing!

William Walker is the 'Winchester Diver', who plunged into the sodden foundations of the Cathedral from 1906-11 to replace the logs in peat with cement bags. He didn't manage to reverse the subsidence, though, and the floor slopes here like a non-league football pitch.

The West Window was destroyed in the Civil War, when the Cathedral was used for stables, but the fragments were put back in the window afterwards, just in a different layout – hence the lack of biblical story-telling here today.

Beautiful 12th century wall paintings in the Holy Sepulchre Chapel; and 13th century tiles in the floor nearby.

Make sure you find the Holy Hole, where pilgrims would gain access to St Swithin's bones, without disturbing the monks at prayer.

As you leave by the west door (south aisle) take a look at the list of those lost in the Crimea, sorted by rank of course: drummers, privates, serjeants, and corporals!

The Daily Admission Fee can only be avoided by paying the Annual Admission Pass. £6.50 to get in, but you get a free tour with that.

Coffee?

Baristas Coffee House

81 High Street, Winchester SO23 9AP

@BaristasHighSt

Open

Daily

Best cup of coffee we had in Winchester, and run by a guy who shows that passion, commitment, good communication skills and great customer service are as important to making it in the coffee world as knowledge of the coffee beans themselves!

Tea?

Forte Tea Rooms

78 Parchment Street, Winchester S023 8AT

www.fortetearooms.co.uk

Open

Monday – Saturday

A lovely pot of loose-leaf tea with home-made scones and jam go down very well in this olde worlde tea room. With gold fabric on the ceiling and fans gently blowing the air around you, this has the feel of a tea room somewhere on the Indian sub-continent rather than the heart of Winchester.

WORCESTER CATHEDRAL
– CHRIST & THE BLESSED MARY

King John is buried here – right by the High Altar.

Check out the Worcester Pilgrim in the Crypt: they unearthed his staff and his boots, dating from 1500.

This cathedral does Big: enormous Bishop's cathedra; gigantic Victorian organ (shame it doesn't work!).

This must be one of the biggest chapter houses in the country; it seated 70, though whether they ever got a full house is not certain.

The Beauchamp tomb is colourful. Baron Beauchamp was beheaded on Tower Hill in 1388, but the tomb replaced his head and gave him a couple of lap dogs and a black swan to sit by him in eternity.

No fixed admission fee, but they recommend a donation of £5 and the guided tour costs £3.

Coffee?

Café Aroma

22 Lychgate, Cathedral Plaza Shopping Centre, Worcester WR1 2QS

www.cafearoma.co.uk

Open

Monday – Saturday

Don't be put off by the anonymous-looking shopping mall where this Worcester coffee shop has its home. Canadian owner Darren has created a home from home for many of his regular customers and you can see why it's first-name-terms all round. Nice cup of coffee and cake by Darren's mother-in-law!

Tea?

The owners of our favourite place for afternoon tea in Worcester sold up in 2013 just before we published, so we have no clear recommendation to make for tea in Worcester.

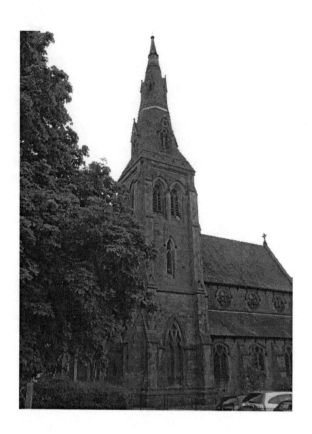

WREXHAM CATHEDRAL – OUR LADY OF SORROWS

Catholic Cathedral built in 1857 by the son of the guy who built the Houses of Parliament in London.

There's a 'relic' – a piece of arm bone – from the body of Welsh Saint Richard Gwyn, who was hung, drawn and quartered in Wrexham's Beast Market in 1584.

No admission fee, just a request for an 'appropriate' donation.

Coffee or tea?

Just Tea & Coffee

6 High Street, Wrexham Ll13 8HP

www.justteaandcoffee.co.uk

Open

Monday – Saturday

A tea merchants occupied this site for several decades at the end of the 19th century, so owner Kim Sheridan has brought things round full circle, but added coffee into the mix for this coffee shop/tea room in the heart of Wrexham. Great little place for a quality cuppa.

YORK MINSTER

The largest Gothic building north of the Alps.

Look out for the alternate red and white roses in the Rose Window above the south door: built to mark the start of the Tudor period when the War of the Roses ended.

Great East Window – when it's there! – is the world's largest area of mediaeval stained glass in a single window: in 2012 Hewlett Packard created a massive curtain copy while it gets repaired.

Spot the heart in the great west window of 1338: known as the 'Heart of Yorkshire' because of its shape.

The mediaeval dragon hanging from the North aisle used to have a pulley attached to lift the font lid.

16th century figures strike the clock on the quarter hour.

The North side of the quire has windows of Yorkshire's saint – St William.

£9 admission charge but you get a guided tour with that, and free entry for 12 months.

Coffee?

Spring Espresso

45 Fossgate, York YO1 9TF

www.springespresso.co.uk
Twitter: @springespresso

Open

Daily

What makes this one of our favourite coffee shops in the UK is not just the quality of the coffee (and the cake), but the positive vibe created by the couple who run the place. Always interested in new ideas in the tea and coffee industry; always keen to give customers the best: Just shows what a difference it makes to be doing something you're passionate about.

Tea?

The Hairy Fig deli and café

39 Fossgate, York YO1 9TF

www.thehairyfig.co.uk

Open

Daily (but closed Sunday January-March)

This tiny tea room in York's best street for independent shops is full of exotic wonders, from the moment you spot the giant Indian tea urn in the window, past all the sweets and oils in the deli, to the little space out the back where you can have top quality loose-leaf tea and wonderful home-baked cakes. Worth waiting even if they're full.

INDEX